Contents

1
Trout 1

2
Lightening the Load 15

3
Zen and the Art of Nymph-Fishing 23

4
The Bass Pond 33

5
Fishing Commandos 43

6
Camp Coffee 53

7
No-See-Ums 61

8
The Fly Collection 69

9
Kazan River Grayling 75

10
Cane Rods 85

11
The Fisher of Small Streams 101

12
Sawhill Portrait 111

13
Headwaters 121

14
Turning Pro 133

15
The Fly Rod 141

16
The Adams Hatch 153

17
Night-fishing 171

18
Cutthroat Pilgrimage 183

19
The Fly Box 201

20
On the Road 213

M C SIMON
1986

TROUT BUM

JOHN GIERACH

Foreword by Gary LaFontaine

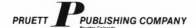
PRUETT PUBLISHING COMPANY
Boulder, Colorado

First Edition

1 2 3 4 5 6 7 8 9

Library of Congress Cataloging-in-Publication Data

Gierach, John, 1946-
  Trout bum.

  1. Trout fishing. I. Title.
SH687.G54   1986   799.1'755   86-4995
ISBN 0-87108-715-4

Printed in the United States of America

Four of these stories — "Zen and the Art of Nymph Fishing,"
"Kazan River Grayling," "Headwaters," and "Turning Pro" —
first appeared in *Flyfishing Magazine*.

"Calling fishing a hobby is like calling brain surgery a job."

— *Paul Schullery*

To the memories of my father, Jack,
and my Uncle Leonard,
who taught me, among other things, how to fish.

Foreword

NO ONE UNDER THE AGE
of thirty qualifies as a trout bum. The whippersnapper living
along a stream, or travelling from river to river, isn't a bum
because he isn't committed to a way of life — he's on an
adventure. He hasn't actually rejected such encumbrances as a
wife, children, and house payments. He just hasn't gotten
around to considering them yet. But the thirty or forty year old
man (or, of course, woman), who commercially ties just enough
flies, guides just enough clients, or sweeps just enough floors so
that he can spend the rest of his hours on the water is a derelict
in the eyes of the world who should confess his sins. Better yet,
he should put that confession into writing so that the rest of us
can cluck over his misspent life.

Ever notice, though, that most of the books in our great
angling tradition have not been written by trout bums? The men
who question perceptively or reminisce lovingly on fly fishing
usually work at full time jobs. Angling for them is often an
escape — an idyllic interlude rather than an everyday fact of life.

But there is a subculture in fly fishing: the trout bum (or
salmon bum, bass bum, or tarpon bum). There is nothing unique

about this — skiing, surfing, and skin diving have their unemployed or barely employed contingents. These people are typically the best at their avocation. And why not? They live for little but their passions.

As a group trout bums are as intelligent, perceptive, talented, and well educated as other fly fishermen. Maybe they make less money per year than most fly fishermen, but that has to be by choice. If "bums" is a negative term it is precisely because such people are poverty stricken not by circumstance but by self-determination. They have decided, for reasons of their own, to pursue the American dream.

Paul Schullery, angling historian and author, has stated, " . . . the modern 'trout bum' is underrepresented in fishing writing."

Why should that be? Is the act of fishing every day itself such a comment that there's no need to put feelings or ideas into words? Why haven't these masters of the sport — friends of mine such as Paul Brown and Wayne Huft qualify — dominated the world of angling magazines and books? They have the poetry in their souls and the strategies in their minds. Who knows the Henry's Fork better than Paul? Who understands the Missouri as fully as Wayne? Not any weekend angler like me — or most of us fly fishermen.

If the greatest philosophical question is "Why", then the only answer broad enough to cover it is "Why not." Trout bums avoid the societal pressures to lead normal lives by answering, "Why not fly fish?" To them, at least, the chance of being a corporation president, a real estate magnate, or a media star pales against the chance to spend a day on the stream. Fair enough (so who's jealous of the s.o.b. s anyway?).

It's obvious why trout bums are underrepresented in angling literature. Writing is so often an act of ego, and anyone who cares so little about what the world thinks of him isn't going to be the moiling mass of insecurities that drives a person after glory. When a trout bum writes it is for money (enough, at least, to let him fish most of the time); when a trout bum writes well it is because he is a craftsman, taking pride (not falsely — not inflated) in his skill as a wordsmith. Writers who are prolific without being hackneyed are all too rare — for me at least the first ones who come to mind are Charles Waterman, Gerald Almy, and John Gierach.

My task here is to assure the readers about John Gierach's qualifications for writing this book. No problem — he's a bum. He's the type that every father worries about his daughter bringing home.

There's a magnificent streak of independence in John. That (along with an obvious love of trout fishing) lets him lead a lifestyle that makes being on the water a priority. He's a real fly fisherman; not an armchair observer who reports on other anglers' exploits or parrots other anglers' ideas.

Last spring we spent a week together on the Blackfoot Reservation in northern Montana. There were no fancy accommodations or posh eateries — there wasn't even a reliable source for angling information. We bounced over dirt roads and flogged prairie potholes day after day. Each night we spread out wet equipment and clothing, hoping it would dry by morning, and ate cold snacks before bedtime. Every frosty dawn we scrambled out again after the elusive trophy trout.

The rains came and broke the spring drought. More water fell in five hours one afternoon than had blessed that region in five months — and it fell on us. It stirred up the rainbows of the rich lakes, though, so when the old Indian stopped us and said, "I'm a medicine man and it's going to rain for five days straight," we didn't know whether to consider it a curse or a promise.

Only one other fisherman came that evening to Kipps Lake, and he sat in his car and watched his propped-up bait rod. The rain began right away, steady enough even at first to make us hunch down in our slickers. The storm ballooned into a downpour, and the wind, a blow unimpeded by trees or hills out there, pushed the drops ahead, harder and harder, until the sheet-water pounded us in 30 to 40 mile per hour gusts. It got so bad that the man in the car couldn't take it anymore and he left. We stayed.

We finally figured out enough about Kipps Lake to catch some of its huge rainbows. My first trout of the following day, a 6-pound fish, impressed us. John's first trout, an 8-pound hen, so young, with a hump of fat over its back, awed us.

Those hours could have been wiled away in a bar (there was one just up the road) and no one would have blamed us. But John never considered it, or at least he never mentioned it. He was there to fish. He had that will of a man who works the water every day; who takes whatever weather arises and catches trout anyway — a trout bum with a western flavor.

John is such a splendid example of a trout bum, and everything unique and free about such anglers, that it's a shame he can't stay that way forever. He's too good a writer to escape success. Worse still, he's so conscientious, turning in polished pieces on time, that magazine and book editors won't stop heaping assignments on him.

By writing books he is gaining too much status as an authority (that's what books, much more so than articles, do for an author). He started with *Fly Fishing the High Country*, a small but very informative volume, and has now produced *Trout Bum*, the kind of philosophical and humorous naturalism that could turn him into a cult figure (a Thoreau in baggy waders).

My favorite pieces include both funny and thoughtful parts of the book. It's going to be hard for people not to chuckle over a chapter like "Zen and the Art of Nymph Fishing," and difficult for readers not to think long afterwards about a piece like "The Fly Rod." This book is going to convert a lot more fishermen into devoted Gierach fans.

It would be sad if on our next trip to the reservation John drove up in a 40-foot Winnebago; or had his film crews there for a television show; or insisted on displaying his Gierach designer waders. Somehow the thought of him chilling his wine in the muck of Kipps Lake doesn't sound as much fun as a tepid can of beer and a Twinkie after a day of dog-crazy flogging.

My bet is that his growing reputation isn't going to change John too much. He may weaken a bit under the pressure from editors and produce more articles and books, but his sense of craftsmanship will insure the quality of his writing. And nothing is likely to lessen his intensity on the water, stemming as it does from an instinctive fascination with fish. He'll stay a trout bum as long as he appreciates the freedom he has to live his angling life on a day to day basis.

—Gary LaFontaine
1986

CHAPTER ONE

Trout

LET'S SAY YOU'RE
nymph-fishing on Colorado's South Platte River. You've hiked
up into the canyon where those deliciously deep potholes are —
the big-fish water — but have found that today the trout are
working the shallow, fast runs. It took you two hours to figure
that out, but it's a good sign. They're hungry and, as your
partner says, they are "looking up." You're fishing a scud
pattern, not *the* scud pattern, but one you worked out yourself.
The differences are minute but are enough to make it your fly
and you are catching fish on it, which is highly satisfactory.

You're working the near edge of a fast rip about thirty yards
above a strong plunge pool, flipping the weighted nymph rig
upstream and following its descent with the rod tip. Your
concentration is imperfect as you toy with the idea that this is
okay, a fascinating and demanding way to fish, actually, but that
too many days of it in a row could make you homesick for the
easy grace of real fly-casting.

At the little jiggle in the leader that was just a hair too intelligent looking to be nothing but current or a rock, you raise the rod to set the hook, and there's weight. And then there's movement — it's a fish.

It's a big fish, not wiggling, but boring, shaking its head in puzzlement and aggravation, but not in fear. It's impressive.

Almost lazily, the trout rises from the bottom into the faster current near the surface, rolls into the rip, and is off downstream. What you feel is more weight than fight, and the wings of panic begin to flutter around your throat. This is the once- or twice-a-year "oh-shit" fish. You should have tried to catch a glimpse of him when he turned — the only glimpse you may get — but it all happened so fast. No it didn't. It actually happened rather slowly, almost lazily, as you just pointed out.

You are careful (too careful? not careful enough?). The hook is a stout, heavy-wire number 10, but the tippet is only a 5x, about 4-pound test. The rod is an 8½-foot cane with plenty of backbone in the butt, but with a nicely sensitive tip (catalog talk, but true). The drag on the reel is set light, and line is leaving it smoothly. You drop the rod to half-mast to give the fish his head and are, in fact, doing everything right. It's hopeless.

The trout is far downstream now, on the far side of the rip and the plunge, but the local topography makes it impossible for you to follow. The line is bellied, no longer pointing at the fish.

At some point you are struck by the knowledge that the trout — that enormous trout — is no longer attached to you and all your expensive tackle, though you missed the exact moment of separation. You reel in to find that he did not throw the hook but broke you off fairly against the weight of the river. You get a mental snapshot of your fly hanging in the hooked jaw of a heavy . . . what? A rainbow? More likely a brown. You'll never know.

Losing a fish like that is hard. Sure, you were going to release him anyway, but that's not the point. The plan was to be magnanimous in victory. You ask yourself, was it my fault? A typically analytical question. You can avoid it with poetry of the "it's just nice to be out fishing" variety, or you can soften it with the many levels of technical evasion, but there's finally only one answer: of course it was your fault, who else's fault would it be?

Your partner is out of sight and, although you would have hollered and screamed for him and his camera had you landed the fish, it's not even worth going to find him, now. When you finally meet in the course of leapfrogging down the canyon, you'll say that a while ago you executed an L.D.R. (long distance release) on a hawg, which will summarize the event as well as anything else you could say.

A trout, on this continent at least, is a rainbow, golden, brookie, brown, cutthroat, or some subspecies or hybrid of the above, though every fly-fisher is secretly delighted that the brook trout isn't a trout at all, but rather a kind of char, not that it matters.

Much is actually known about trout and much more is suspected. The serious fly-fisherman's knowledge of these fish draws heavily on science, especially the easygoing, slightly bemused, English-style naturalism of the last century, but it periodically leaves the bare facts behind to take long voyages into anthropomorphism and sheer poetry. Trout are said to be angry, curious, shy, belligerent, or whatever; or it's suggested that when one takes your Adams with a different rise form than he's using on the Blue-winged Olives, he "thought" it was a caddis fly. Cold science tells us that a trout's pea-sized brain is not capable of anything like reason or emotion. That's probably true enough, but in the defense of creative thinking, I have a comment and a question: actions speak louder than words and, if they're so dumb, how come they can be so hard to catch?

The myth of the smart trout was invented by fishermen as a kind of implied self-aggrandizement. To be unable to hook the wise old brown trout is one thing, but to be outsmarted by some slimy, cold-blooded, subreptilian creature with only the dullest glimmerings of awareness is, if not degrading, then at least something you don't want spread around. Trout are smart, boy, real smart.

The way we perceive trout is probably as faulty, from a factual standpoint, as the way they see us, but our folksy ideas about them are useful and are, in that sense, correct. If you tie a streamer fly and fish it in a way designed to make spawning brown trout "mad" and, in the course of events, manage to hook a few fish, then those fish were, by God, mad. End of discussion.

Let's say a fisheries biologist tells you that his studies, and the studies of others, demonstrate that brook trout are not piscivorous; that is, they don't eat other fish. To that you counter that you have caught countless brook trout on streamers (fish imitations), that many of the now-standard American streamer patterns were developed around the wild brook trout fisheries of the East, and that, further, fly-fishermen have believed brook trout to be fish-eaters for nigh on these many generations.

"Well," he says, "we all know brookies are stupid."

Thank you, Mister Science.

Finally, the things fishermen know about trout aren't facts but articles of faith. Brook trout may or may not eat fish, but they bite streamers. You can't even use the scientific method because the results of field testing are always suspect. There are too many variables and the next guy to come along may well prove an opposing theory beyond the shadow of a doubt.

The hatch is the Blue-winged Olive so common in the West. It's a perfect emergence from the fly-fisher's point of view: heavy enough to move all but the very largest of the trout but not so heavy that your pitiful imitation is lost in such a crowd of bugs that the surface of the stream seems fuzzy. Oh yes, hatches can be too good.

When the rise began you fished a #18 dark nymph pattern squeezed wet so it would drift just a fraction of an inch below the surface. This copies the emerging nymph at that point where it has reached the surface but has not yet hatched into the winged fly. Early on in the hatch, these are the bugs that are the most readily available to the fish, the ones they're probably taking even though at first glance it looks like they're rising to dry flies. The difference in position between an emerging nymph and a floating fly is the almost nonexistent thickness of the surface film of the water, and there is often zero difference between the trouts' rise forms.

When the hatch progresses to the point where there are more winged flies on the water than emerging nymphs, you switch to the dry fly, only a few minutes after most of the trout have. There are two mayflies on the water now, identical except that one is about a size 18 and the other, the more numerous, is more like a #22. The larger is the *Baetis* and the smaller is the *Pseudocloeon.* You heard that from the local expert and looked up the spellings in *Hatches,* by Caucci and Nastasi. It sounds good, but what it means is that you fish either the Blue-winged Olive or the Adams in a size 20, to split the difference.

The fish are an almost uniform 14 to 16 inches — rainbows with a strong silvery cast to them, bodies fatter than most stream fish, with tiny little heads. They are wild and healthy, and you would drive five times farther than you did to fish here.

They're rising everywhere now. In the slower water they're dancing and darting, suspending for a few seconds now and then as if to catch their breath. They will move several inches for your fly, taking it matter-of-factly, completely fooled, but leaving you only a single, precise instant that won't be too early or too late to strike. This has you wound up like the E string on a pawn shop guitar.

In the faster water they are all but invisible, but they're out there because there are enough bugs to make them buck the current. They come up from the bottom through two feet of water, taking the fly with such grace and lack of hesitation that the little blip on the surface seems unconnected with that fluid arc of greenish, pinkish, silvery light in the riffle.

You are on, hot, wired. You've caught so many trout that the occasional missed strike is a little joke between you and the fish. This is the exception rather than the rule — the time when everything comes together — but it feels comfortable, like it happens all the time. A hint of greed creeps in. You would like, maybe, a little bigger trout, and to that end you work the far bank. Still, though the trout are now almost part of a process rather than individual victories, you admire each one momentarily before releasing it and going confidently for another.

It's late in the hatch now. Most of the river is in shadow, and the remaining light has a golden, autumnal cast to it. The little rusty-brownish spinners could come on now. This could last. But it's too perfect; it *can't* last.

Trout are wonderfully hydrodynamic creatures who can dart and hover in currents in which we humans have trouble just keeping our footing. They are torpedo shaped, designed for moving water, and behave like eye witnesses say U.F.O.s do, with sudden stops from high speeds, ninety-degree turns, such sudden accelerations that they seem to just vanish. They seem delicate at times but will turn around and flourish in conditions that look impossibly harsh. They like things clean and cold.

They are brilliantly, often outrageously, colored (the wild ones, anyway) and are a pure and simple joy to behold, though they can be damned hard to see in the water. Even the most gorgeously colored fish are as dark and mottled on the back as the finest U.S. Army-issue jungle camouflage to hide them from predators from above: herons, kingfishers, ospreys, and — only recently in evolutionary terms — you and me. Then there are those rare times when the light and everything else is just right, when they're as exposed as birds in the sky, in open water under bright sun as if they were in paradise. At such times they can look black. You feel like a voyeur, delighted with a view of something you have no right to see; but don't feel too guilty — they'll spook at your first cast.

In one sense trout are perfectly adapted working parts of a stream, a way of turning water, sunlight, oxygen, and protein into consciousness. They feed on the aquatic insects when those bugs are active, and they all but shut down metabolically when they're not. They find glitches in the current where, even in the wildest water, they can lounge indefinitely by now and then lazily paddling a pectoral fin. They have the flawless competence that even the lower mammals have lost by getting to be too smart. They operate at the edges of things: fast and slow currents, deep and shallow water, air and stream, light and darkness, and the angler who understands that is well on his way to knowing what he's doing.

In another sense, trout are so incongruously pretty as to seem otherworldly: that metallic brightness, the pinks and oranges and yellows — and the spots. One of the finest things about catching a trout is being able to turn it sideways and just look at it. How can so much color and vibrancy be generated by clear water, gray rocks, and brown bugs? Trout are among those creatures who are one hell of a lot prettier than they need to be. They can get you to wondering about the hidden workings of reality.

Releasing trout is a difficult idea to get hold of at first. It doesn't seem to make sense. You want the meat; you want the *proof*.

In the beginning, catching a trout on a fly is one of those things you have to do before you actually come to believe it's possible. Those first maddening weeks or months with a fly rod make other fly-casters seem like the guy in the circus who can put the soles of his feet flat on the top of his head. Sure, *he* can do it. If you don't flip out and go back to the spinning rod, you eventually find that it can be done, though the gap between the first time you take trout on a fly rod and the second time can be so wide you come to wonder if it ever really happened. It's easy to lose the clarity of that initial vision. You hear it all the time: "I tried fly-fishing; couldn't get the hang of it."

You keep the early trout (anyone who doesn't is too saintly to be normal) but in time you begin to see the virtue of releasing the wild fish. The logic is infallible: if you kill him, he's gone; if you release him, he's still there. You can think of it in terms of recycling, low impact, all the properly futuristic phrases.

With some practice it's easy to do correctly. Smaller trout can be landed quickly — the barbless hook is turned out with a practiced motion of the wrist, and it darts away, baffled but unharmed. You haven't lifted him from the water or even touched him.

Larger fish require more handling. You're careful not to lift them by the gill covers or squeeze them too much, causing internal damage. A landing net with a soft cotton-mesh bag helps. Big fish played to exhaustion on tackle that's unavoidably too light are carefully resuscitated (held gently in the current and pumped until they get their wind back and can swim off under their own steam). They seem dazed, and you know that if they were stressed too much, with too much lactic acid built up in their systems, they'll eventually die. It's something to wonder about. Some of your released fish have probably expired later, but you don't know enough about it to determine the actual medical condition of any particular one.

It begins to feel good, the heft and muscle tension of a bright, pretty, live trout held lightly in the cold water. It's like a mild electric shock without the pain. Finally, there's not even an instant of remorse when they dart away. At some point your former values change ends; the bigger the trout, the more satisfying the release. Having all but lost your taste for fish, you

begin to release everything — wild fish, stockers, stunted brook
trout, whitefish, bluegills — with an air of righteousness that
pains many of those around you.

At some point you become an absolute snot about it. You are
incensed that even staunch antihunters aren't bothered by the
killing of fish, that vegetarians will bend the rules for seafood.
This, you come to realize, is because trout are not seen as cute
by the general population, though of course they are wrong. You
begin to feel misunderstood.

That feeling can go on for years, and in some anglers it
calcifies into the belief that killing a trout is murder. But maybe
one day, without giving it much thought, you go down to the
reservoir, after having spotted the hatchery truck there in the
morning, and bag a limit of stockers (pale, sickly-looking things
with faint purplish stripes where the pink stripe would be on a
wild rainbow). It doesn't feel half bad.

Breaded with yellow cornmeal and flour and fried in butter,
they're okay, not unlike fishsticks, but with a livery undertaste.

That same season, or perhaps the next, you take a brace of
wild fish for what you refer to as a "ceremonial" camp dinner,
carefully pointing out that they are small brook trout from
overpopulated water. They taste good. They taste wonderful.

You come to realize that you have to kill some now and then
because this whole business of studying, stalking, outsmarting,
and overpowering game is *about* death and killing. Take two
(three, if they're small) coldly and efficiently, and if you
comment on it at all, say something like, "That there is a nice
mess of fish."

You still release most of the trout you catch, even in waters
where that's not the law, but it's no longer a public gesture. Now
it's just what pleases you. When they're big and pretty, you take
a photograph, with Kodachrome for the hot colors.

The river was the Henry's Fork in Southern Idaho, at a place

that I have been politely asked not to describe. I'll try not to. It's
not far upstream from the spot where Archie (A. K.) Best and I
saw a yard-long rainbow try to eat a blackbird who was standing
at the end of a sweeper picking off Brown Drakes. Honest.
Biggest trout either of us had ever seen. The bird got away.

This was the following year and, hunting for the Brown Drake
hatch that never materialized, we located another big trout,
maybe 25 inches long (maybe longer, it's hard to tell), who was
unbelievably feeding on #18 Pale Morning Dun spinners. Only
on a bug factory like the Henry's Fork would a fish of that size
still be interested in little mayflies. We decided it would be great
fun to hook a trout like that on a dry fly and, say, a 5x tippet. I
say "hook." We never discussed how we'd land it and I doubt
either of us seriously considered it could be done. Still, with all
that open water, slow current, and plenty of backing . . . It
would have been something.

It was early June. The Pale Morning Duns were coming off,
with simultaneous spinner falls and a smattering of Green Drakes
that the fish would switch to when they showed up. Some locals
and some hot-dog tourists said the fishing was "slow." A. K. and
I wondered what the hell they wanted.

By day we fished in the crowd, sometimes taking an afternoon
break to hit the campground, ease out, sip coffee, tie some flies.
One day we went up to another stream and caught some little
rainbows and brookies for lunch. As we do on the Henry's Fork,
we discussed the possibility of taking a day and hitting the
Madison or the Teton, or even the Warm River, but never went.
We were Henry's Fork junkies on a typical extended trip.

By night (early evening, actually) we would drive to a certain
turnoff and then walk to a certain spot where the impossibly big
rainbow would be rising to the spinner fall like clockwork. We
had Rusty Spinners, Cream Spinners, quill-bodied and dubbed-
bodied spinners, spinners with poly wings and hackle-tip wings
and clipped-hackle wings, and, for later, Michigan Chocolate
spinners for that sharp, dark silhouette against the night sky.

We were fishing rods we'd each built up from identical blanks, old 9-foot, 6-weight waterseals. They were heavy rods, but slow and powerful, just what one would need to land that heavy a trout on a little fly and light tippet. We'd thought this out very well.

For five, maybe six, nights we showed up regularly at that spot and returned to the campground just as the last few friendship fires were down to coals. It would be too late to start anything, so we'd sit on the ground around our cold fire pit, sipping a beer before turning in and muttering arcanely about the fish, the flies, the insects, leader diameters, knots, and the hoped-for commencement of the Brown Drake hatch that we thought might give us a real crack at *The Trout*. If he (she, probably, but I can't help thinking of big trout as masculine) was taking the little spinners, he'd surely move for the huge #10 Drakes. The big flies would help, and their nighttime emergence and large size would let us go to heavier leaders. In our quiet madness we actually tried to quantify how much of an advantage that would give us. It was time. It could happen any night now. Exactly one year ago the hatch had been on.

Our colleagues at the campground figured we had something going — probably fishwise, possibly womanwise — but, although they sometimes hedged around it a little, they never actually came out and asked. Night-fishers are seen as a distinctly antisocial breed and are best not pushed.

We would take turns casting to *The Trout*, alternating who started first on successive nights. We were perfect gentlemen about it, wishing each other well with complete unselfishness, and then cringing with covetous greed as the other guy worked the fish. One night I broke down and fished a big, weighted Brown Drake nymph and then, later, an enormous streamer on an Ox leader. Not even a bump. A.K. stayed righteous with the dry fly.

Another night a mackenzie boat with a guide and two sports came down from upriver. The guide obviously knew about the

fish and wanted to put his clients over it, either because he
thought they were good enough to do some business or just to
blow their minds. He was pulling for the channel when he
spotted me casting from a kneeling crouch and A. K. sitting
cross-legged next to me waiting for me to relinquish my turn.

The guide gave us only the briefest sour look and then
delivered the obligatory we're-all-in-this-together-good-luck wave.

Two turkeys on the big trout. Damn!

During the course of those evenings we each hooked that fish
once and were each summarily, almost casually, broken off,
causing our estimation of his size to be revised upwards to the
point where inches and pounds became meaningless — a fish of
which dreams are made, known to the local guides.

You could hear him rising through the layered silence of the
stream: "GLUP!" He'd start rising late, when the spinner fall was
down nicely and the smaller fish were already working.

The smaller fish. We caught a few of those, measuring up to
19 and 22 inches, our two largest. Such is the capacity of the
human mind to compare one thing to another, thus missing the
moment and thinking of a 22-inch trout as a little fish.

Exactly what a trout is, not to mention its considerable
significance, is difficult to convey to someone who doesn't fish
for them with a fly rod. There's the biology and taxonomy,
photographs, paintings, and the long history of the sport, but
what the nonangler is incapable of grasping is that, although
individual fish clearly exist, *The Trout* remains a legendary
creature. I'm talking about those incredible fish that we see but
can't catch, or don't even see but still believe in. The *big* trout —
another concept the nonfisherman thinks he understands but
doesn't.

What constitutes a big trout is a relative thing, regardless of
the efforts of some to make it otherwise. You'll now and then
hear a fly-fisher say a trout isn't really big until it's 20 inches

long, a statement I invariably take to be jet-set bullshit, although I'll grant you that 20 inches is a nice, round figure. Fisheries managers often refuse to consider a piece of water as gold medal (or blue ribbon, or whatever) unless it demonstrably contains x percentage of trout over x inches in length. The magazines are filled with photos of huge, dripping trout, the ones you'll catch if you'll only master the following technique.

In another camp are the fishermen who claim not to care how big a trout is. "It's the challenge," they'll say, "the flies, the casting, the manner and method. Nothing wrong with a foot-long trout. Oh, and the scenery, and the birds singing, etc." I use that line myself and, like most of us, I sincerely believe it, act upon it regularly, and am happy, but tell me you know where the hawgs are and I'll follow you through hell.

Fly-fishing for trout is a sport that depends not so much on catching the fish as on their mere presence and on the fact that you do, now and again, catch some. As for their size, the bigger they are, the better, to be honest about it, though all that stuff about the manner and the method and the birds singing isn't entirely compensatory.

CHAPTER TWO

Lightening the Load

I TOOK UP FLY-FISHING
long enough ago that I don't remember exactly when it was, but
I remember I had the novice's ready-made fascination with all
the mysterious gear and gadgets. In fact, it was probably the
exotic tackle and accoutrements that first attracted me to the
sport. I had previously fished with what I now think of as
"nonfly" tackle, but the stuff fly-fishermen carried was both
beautiful and serious looking at the same time — like a big,
jangling ring of keys to a different reality. I was clearly hooked
on the ambiance before I even got started, which is *why* I got
started in the first place.

Of course, like all such things, it was more complicated than I
first imagined. I remember walking into a store and announcing
that I'd come to buy a fly rod.

"What kind?" asked the guy behind the counter.

"You mean there are different kinds?"

I asked for a regular-old, garden-variety fly rod and ended up
with a fiberglass 7½-footer for a #6 line fitted with a Pflueger

Medalist reel. I passed up the one you could convert to a
spinning rod by doing some fancy footwork with the reel seat.
After all, I was a purist.

It took me a few trips to the store and a bit more money than
I'd planned on — an ominous sign of things to come — but
soon I had what I then considered to be the full getup: a small,
inexpensive, flimsy vest, some leader material, a bottle of
mosquito repellent, a pair of Taiwanese ditchboots, and a box of
about a dozen flies, also from somewhere in the Third World.
The flies were all nice and big and real pretty.

At first I thought I was in business, but it wasn't long before I
started feeling half naked next to the archetypal properly attired
fly-fisherman I'd meet on the streams. Some of these guys were
pretty impressive; they looked like combinations of tackle stores,
biology labs, and hospital emergency wards. The rattling,
clanking sound they made when they walked had an authoritative
ring to it, and most of them seemed to have evolved elaborate
personal systems for balancing a strung-up fly rod, fly box,
forceps, micrometer (you can't trust the factory measurements
on this tippet material, you know), imported English
scissor/pliers, etc.

They'd descend on the stream like information-gathering
modules, sprouting collection nets, specimen bottles, and stream
thermometers, and could often be heard muttering to each other
in some foreign language I later discovered to be Latin: "Clearly
one of the large Ephemerella, probably the doddsi, though
possibly the glacialis, easily mistaken for the E. grandis. Better tie
on an Adams."

The only Latin I could remember from college was *cogito ergo
sum* ("I think, therefore I am"), I think.

The clincher was that most of these guys seemed to catch
more trout than I did, and the only obvious difference between
us was all that equipment. I began to suffer from voidophobia —
the unreasoning fear of empty vest pockets. I didn't know
exactly what I needed, but I clearly needed a lot of stuff, enough

stuff to make me clank and rattle when I walked, to strain the single-stitched seams of my cheap vest, enough to put me in the same league with the guys who were catching all the fish.

By this time I'd figured out there were shops that dealt exclusively in fly tackle. (I'd bought my first gear at a place that also sold tires, garden tools, school supplies, Mexican felt paintings, and hot dogs.) I've since worked in fly shops and have cringed to see myself in some of the rosy-cheeked types who came in and asked things like, "What size fly do I need to catch a 20-inch brown?" or "How do I tie this little bitty fly to this big fat fly line?"

"Well . . . you need a leader."

"A what?"

A clerk in the average fly shop spends half his time patiently leading people from the middle back to somewhere near the beginning.

Luckily, I happened to walk into the now-defunct Hank Roberts shop on Walnut Street in Boulder, Colorado. Had I stumbled into the clutches of an unscrupulous tackle dealer, I could easily have been fleeced for my life savings, such as they were. I wanted *stuff*, lots of it.

As it was, I was sold a few flies (Adamses and Hares Ears), a tapered leader and some tippet material, and one of those fancy double-tapered lines to replace my level #6. I was even treated to a free casting lesson out in the parking lot.

"Look, you're not throwing a rock, you're casting a fly rod. Let the rod do the work."

"Yeah, right, oof, oof, oof."

"And by the way, when you get a chance, you might want to get yourself a *decent* rod."

There were some decent rods back inside, rods with names like Leonard, Thomas & Thomas, and Orvis on them. A few cost more than the pickup truck I was driving, some of the gray smoke from which was still drifting through the open front door. Some of them were made from some kind of blonde-colored wood that was sawed up into six strips.

"Split cane."

"Huh?"

"Bamboo."

"Oh, right, I had a bamboo rod when I was a kid."

"(sigh)"

I didn't know it then, but I'd been treated well. Still, I was disappointed that I didn't clank and rattle any more than I did before, and after spending a fair piece of change, too.

I started reading magazines, and then books on the subject. There was this guy named Ernest something (not Hemingway) who seemed to know a lot about bugs. Well and good, but what size fly do I need to catch a 20-inch brown?

Slowly, gradually, I began to realize what I needed. (In the language of fly-fishing, "need" is roughly synonymous with "want.") I needed forceps, scissor/pliers, tweezers (no telling what for), enough leader material to build a hand-tied tapered leader from the butt down, fingernail clippers with a folding knife blade that said "Henry's Fork Anglers/Last Chance, Idaho" on them (only a rank amateur buys his clippers at a drug store), a combination tape measure and scale, stomach pump, bug net, specimen bottles, fly boxes, leader stretchers, waterproof match holder, wader patch kit, flashlight, two types each of fly float and fly sink, and, well . . .

I learned that getting oneself properly outfitted wasn't cheap, or even acceptable in some circles. I was still married to my second wife at the time, and I can recall the long, serious discussions over the kitchen table at two o'clock in the morning over the relative values of three-hundred dollars' worth of fly tackle (plus eighty dollars for a bigger vest to carry it all in) and, say, getting the leak in the roof fixed.

The fact that I'm single now only illustrates that a sportsman of my caliber can't possibly live with someone whose ducks aren't in a row. She used to say, "You never take me anywhere!" and I'd answer calmly, logically, "I took you fishing just last month."

A friend once asked, "How come a guy who dresses in rags and drives a smoky old pickup can afford such snazzy tackle?"

"It should be obvious."

The final blow came when I took up fly tying. I did it to save money at first (sixty-five cents each for dry flies then) but soon expanded to where I had more money in tying materials and tools than I'd ever have spent on flies and needed the better part of a room to set up shop. Luckily the old sewing room was empty. I got a cold-water aquarium so I could raise trout-stream insects for study and placed it under the leak in the roof.

I tied flies more or less daily, filling box after box, first with standards and then with examples of every pattern that appeared in any magazine under the heading "new." My new vest ("I want the biggest one with the most pockets; money is no object") began to look pregnant. I had arrived.

Somewhere along the line I discovered retractor pins and added, to my repertoire of clanks and rattles, a very professional sounding "zzzzzzup, chunk."

Also somewhere along the line (coincidentally, I think) I began to catch some trout, a circumstance that branded my pig-greed for tackle, flies, and gadgets deeply on my subconscious.

Then something happened. A couple of seasons ago I began to notice two things: I was having to make several trips out to the truck to load the gear for a single afternoon's fishing, and I was developing a chronic backache.

I also began to lose things. I'd be out on the stream with trout rising all around me, rummaging through the vest looking for a #14 Adams the way you can wander around in an old-time hardward store for hours looking for something as basic as a can opener. During the search I would invariably come across some piece of gear that I didn't even recognize. It got me thinking.

The following winter, during what would turn out to be the heaviest snowfall in fifty years, I sat down to the annual ritual of going over the gear: oiling reels, cleaning lines, rebuilding leaders, etc. Everything but washing the vest. I'd been led to believe that washing a fly vest is bad luck, and when I broke down and did it once, I ended up laundering a perfectly good stream thermometer down to ground glass and lodging a Gray Ghost in the lint trap.

I did clean *out* the vest, however, and got a pile of stuff that covered the kitchen table and dribbled onto the floor in several places. I separated my fly boxes from the pile and found that, out of nine boxes, only about a dozen compartments were anywhere near empty. Hmmmmm . . .

Many of the other compartments (or rows of clips) held flies I couldn't remember tying or even having seen before: things with burned wings, extended bodies, eyeballs, legs with knees, ankles, and feet — flies that had apparently never been wet.

I sat down then and carefully sorted out every fly, tool, and gadget I couldn't remember having used during the last season. The small pile that was left over very much resembled the handful of gear I'd started with years before. Ah-ha!

The three-foot-tall stack of catalogs in the corner (at that point I was on the mailing list for every catalog in the English language in which the word "fish" appeared) seemed to cringe and let out a little whimper. The tackle industry needn't have worried, though. The empty vest looked like the shed skin of a fat snake lying there on the floor, so I impulsively grabbed the top catalog and ordered a light, four-pocketed fishing shirt. As John Updike said, "America teaches its children that every passion can be transmuted into an occasion to buy."

So now, at least on short trips to waters I know well, I've been wearing the fishing shirt with one fly box, clippers, fly floatant, and three spools of leader material. The exact fly selection doesn't matter here. There are six patterns in assorted sizes, pretty much the same ones we've all read about in all the "My Favorite Six Flies" articles that have ever been published. In late summer I toss in a couple of hoppers, early and late in the season I add a small box of midges, and sometimes there are some streamers. It changes a little from time to time because that's what fly selections do, but it doesn't change much.

Do I ever get caught short? Sure, now and then, but no shorter and no more often than I did when I carried every item of tackle known to man. It's just a different challenge — to try to see how little you can get away with instead of how much you can carry, to replace the majority of that gear with skill and knowledge, if that doesn't sound too stuck-up. I'm catching at least as many trout as I did before, maybe even a few more, because I'm forcing myself to learn how to fish.

No, I haven't given the other fly boxes or the vest away and I probably never will. I carry the full catastrophe to all strange waters as well as to familiar ones where tame trout rise selectively to heavy hatches of bugs. I recently wore the vest on a trip to New Mexico's San Juan River but, even though I tied some flies for the trip and bought some more on the spot (San Juan Worms, they were called), I took all my fish with patterns that I carry in the fishing shirt. Interesting. There may come a day . . . But for now, I'm keeping the stuff — all of it.

Still, this season I've worn the fishing shirt almost exclusively on waters with which I'm familiar. Sometimes I try to tell myself that I'm just so damned good now, I don't need all that other stuff anymore, but that's just normal angler's egotism. The fact is, I'm doing what I've always done and am beginning to see that I *never* needed the other stuff.

The pared-down version of my fly tackle fits neatly in the two breast pockets of the fishing shirt, leaving the bottom pockets (not to mention the "cargo pouch" in the back) empty. To tell you the truth, those unused spaces sometimes give me mild attacks of voidophobia, but I think I'll be okay in time. The shirt itself is comfortable now, nicely broken in. It even has a tar stain on it that I got while fixing that leak in the roof.

CHAPTER THREE

Zen and the Art of Nymph-Fishing

STUDENT: "MASTER,
how does one tell when the trout has taken the fly?"
Master: "The moon is reflected in the still pond, my son."

The man who taught me to nymph-fish isn't a Zen master and
he doesn't come up with answers like that very often. Instead he
says things that, in Twentieth-Century America, amount to the
same thing:
Student: "So, how do you tell when you get a strike?"
Master: "How much did you pay for that reel?"
The actual mechanics of short-line nymph-fishing aren't very
complicated or difficult — you really don't even have to know
how to properly cast a flyrod — but detecting the strike of an
unseen trout to an unseen fly is one of the hardest things a fly-
fisher will ever have to learn. It's a skill that relies largely on
intuition and the ability to see things that aren't immediately
evident, or rather, to see things that are evident *in their own way.*

I learned how to fish with nymphs in the deep, clear plunge pools of the South Platte River, and my teacher was Ed Engle, a gentleman who was nearing legendary status on the Platte before he moved south to other mountains and rivers. Ed works for the U.S. Forest Service now and is one of those guys who has lived, worked, and played in the woods for a long, long time. He has both a factual and an intuitive understanding of things in the outdoors and an easygoing way of dealing with them. He also pays as much attention to his boots and socks as he does to all his other gear combined, the mark of a true outdoorsman. Ed has a degree in biology from the University of Colorado but was known around Boulder in his college days as a poet.

When Ed and I first fished the Platte together, I was deep into what I now consider to be my "tweed-and-cane" period — spending much more time and money than I could afford collecting snazzy tackle, tying flies with every minute anatomical feature that could be crammed onto a hook, and reading (though not necessarily understanding) every volume on entomology I could lay my hands on. I wanted to be just like those guys who write for the magazines.

Although Ed and I had taken up fly-fishing at about the same time, he had somehow managed to retain a kind of innocence about it, while I had gotten — or had *tried* to get — very technical. His tackle was spartan, basic, what I considered then to be just barely adequate: rod, reel, line, a few spools of monofilament, and, worst of all, a single fly box containing a handful of patterns, all lacking, as Dave Whitlock puts it, "eyeballs, elbows, and arseholes."

He also prowled the streams wearing faded overalls and a baseball cap advertising a well-known manufacturer of earth-moving equipment, and he spat gobs of evil-looking tobacco juice. He was not, and is not today, your typical uptown fly-fisherman (you'll never see him modeling camouflage sport coats in any catalog). The fact that he regularly caught more and bigger trout than I did was my first hint that I might be overlooking something basic.

What Ed has is simple fish sense — *game* sense — the thing all great hunters and fishermen have had. It isn't exactly knowledge as we usually think of it, though knowledge doesn't seem to hurt it any; nor is it extrasensory perception, though it sure as hell looks like it at times. A large part of it, I think, is the gut realization that trout (in this case) evolved along with us here on the same planet, from the same primordial goo. They're not alien creatures; they're just like us in most ways, and what they're about is fairly obvious. In fact, the only way trout really differ from us is that they're only as smart as they need to be, whereas we humans tend to be too smart for our own good. Trout don't cloud issues.

Fish sense, applied in the field, is what the old Zen masters would call enlightenment: simply the ability to see what's right there in front of you without having to sift through a lot of thoughts and theories and, yes, expensive fishing tackle. It's the ability to find and catch trout without really knowing (or caring) how you do it. And if those wrinkled old sages back in the Sung Dynasty had spent less time sitting cross-legged in meditation halls and more time fishing for carp in the Yellow River, we'd know a lot more about it today.

Of course, much of what a nymph-fisher needs to know is readily available information. Where do the trout in most streams do the majority of their feeding? On the bottom of deep runs which are, ideally, located below riffles, where they're supplied with a more or less constant flow of nymphs and aerated water. The deep bottom currents are much slower than those nearer the surface, thus allowing the fish the maximum food intake for the least amount of energy spent. Biology.

When the run is more than a few feet deep, you get your hook down there either by fishing a huge stone fly nymph with half a pound of lead for an underbody, or you add weight to the leader in the form of split shot or twist-ons. The weighted rig is cast well upstream of where you suspect the fish to be and is allowed to sink as it drifts downcurrent. You then follow the drift of the nymph with the rod tip — keeping just enough slack out so that the fly achieves something like a dead drift — and watch for a strike. Technique.

"But how do you *tell* when you get a strike?"

"Well, my son, life is like a beanstalk, isn't it?"

The strike to a deep, dead drifted nymph is signaled, if at all, by a very slight bump, jiggle, twitch, jerk, hesitation, wiggle (or whatever else you want to call it) in the floating part of the line or leader and/or by an equally slight movement, flash or shadow on the bottom. G. E. M. Skues described the latter as "that cunning brown wink underwater," referring to brown trout, of course.

That looks fine on paper (it *sounded* fine when Ed explained it to me on the bank of the Family Pool), but in practice it is, at first, almost useless. Viewed through polarized glasses and four feet of moving water, the bottom of a trout stream is nothing *but* winks and movements; moreover, your line does a constant bump and grind on the surface currents. If you're fishing right on the bottom as you should be, you can add to all that the inevitable twitches, bumps, wiggles, etc., caused by your weight ticking on the stream bed.

The first day I actually tried deep nymphing I hooked two fish, both of which were just "there" when I lifted the rod for another cast — by accident, in other words. During that same afternoon, Ed caught countless trout, some of them from spots I'd already fished hard. He assured me I'd get the hang of it.

I'll admit I got a little miffed at Ed early on because he didn't seem to be very helpful. After all, we were friends who went back a long way. We'd been on the road together, hunted and fished together, camped together in mountains and desert, and done other things I won't mention in the interests of brevity and good taste. I'll get the hang of it? Come on.

He wouldn't tell me the secret because there *was* no secret, and I did finally get the hang of it, though it took a while. Whether Ed intended it or not, he taught me how to nymph-fish in the finest Zen tradition: he showed me how to rig the fly with a pair of split shot about a foot up the leader, put me in a good spot, stuffed a wad of chew in his cheek, and stalked off upstream.

It's funny how long you sometimes have to look at a thing before you actually start to see it. You cast. You stare into the water, which is all wiggles, flashes, and refractions, and watch your line bouncing and dancing on the surface currents. You haven't got a clue.

Maybe, after an hour of this, you creep up around the next bend, hide in the bushes, and watch the master for a while. He's perched at the edge of a deep plunge pool, his body cocked forward slightly like a heron stalking a minnow. Each cast is exactly like the last. He lets the line belly out downstream, lobs it upstream with an exaggerated, almost graceful, flip of the rod, and, with his arm extended straight and parallel with the surface, he follows the drift again and again. At first the look on his face seems stern, then it appears to be slightly blissed-out, and then you realize it's, well . . . expressionless.

Occasionally his rod hand and line hand twitch in opposite directions, a motion that raises the rod tip and tightens the line at the same time. About every third or fourth time he does that, the rod bends and jumps. A fish.

He allows himself a lopsided grin and spits a stream of tobacco juice over his shoulder.

With the trout landed and released, he returns to the same spot, his face goes blank, and he begins again: flip, drift, swing; flip, drift, swing. You wade back to your spot muttering to yourself.

One of the classic forms of Zen instruction is the koan, the unsolvable puzzle. The master asks you, "What is the sound of one hand clapping?" or, "A girl is crossing the street. Is she the younger or the older sister?" You sit on a cold stone bench and meditate on that for six months and finally you start to giggle. You're enlightened. Suddenly you can heal the sick, raise the dead, and write poetry. Or maybe you can't do any of those things, but so what?

A good koan would be, "Set the hook on the invisible strike."

I recall days of largely fruitless nymph-fishing on the South Platte — puzzlement, frustration — but the memories are not unpleasant. No good lessons are entirely easy and, anyway, there were the evening rises when a guy could tie on a dry fly and catch trout in a reasonable, civilized way.

Still, I worked at nymphing. I had become determined to set on anything, *anything*, that looked the slightest bit fishy, even though I didn't really know from experience what I was looking for. That had to be what Ed was doing; not even *he* set up on a fish every time.

I struck when the shadow of a raven crossed the stream, when the sun flashed on the water (and when the sun stopped flashing on the water for an instant), when a squirrel dropped a pine cone, when the fly ticked a rock on the bottom, when the leader swirled in an eddy the size of a quarter, when I just, by God, felt like it. Once I set up and hooked a rubbery, waterlogged willow branch and played the thing for five minutes.

The first trout I actually caught (as opposed to those that hooked themselves one way or another) was doing a fair imitation of a largemouth bass. He hit the nymph hard, nailing it a foot out of his feeding lane. He flashed like a mirror under the surface and jerked the line forward a good three inches. I could have been asleep and still hooked that fish, but that's not the point. The point is, I saw the strike, set the hook, and sure enough . . .

Even though that hasn't happened more than a dozen times in the years since, it taught me one thing, or, more properly, it impressed one thing on my subconscious: that there is, however subtle it might be, a certain quick, sure efficiency to the movements of a feeding trout, even when muted by four feet of water and the same length of monofilament. It's something that stands apart from the more random motions of water on line and sun on water, something that indicates a purpose and an intelligence — and that's when you set the hook.

I started catching fish then, not a lot of fish, but enough, and I started seeing what was there. I realized that peripheral vision would easily cover the movements of the leader and line once the neural synapses were trained to detect another intelligence (rather than to just insert tab A into slot B), and I started to just look at the water in the general vicinity of my drift.

The water in a trout stream — ideally, at least — has no color, but it *seems* to have a color. On the South Platte in Cheesman Canyon it's a kind of muddy, but at the same time silvery, green (not coincidentally the same color as many of the mayfly nymphs). The flashing sides of a wild South Platte rainbow are exactly the same color except that there's a hint of the aged beer can to it, a living, and so not quite metallic, feeling to it. Set the hook.

The yellow belly of a mature brown trout is a shade or two darker than butter melting on a perfectly browned pancake, and he shows it when he takes a nymph and then rolls back the three inches to his original lie.

There's an instant of tightness in the normal dance of a leader in current that indicates a trout has mouthed the fly — however briefly or gently — and you can tell, the way you can tell from the sound whether a guitar string has been struck by a musician or say, bumped by the tail of a passing dog.

At some point, the setting of the hook takes on an instinctive quality. At some point you stop thinking, "Hey, I think I just got a hit," or "Gee, that kind of looked like a trout." The wiggle or flash and the jerk in the rod hand seem to happen simultaneously, automatically, the same way you drop a hot frying pan without first having to think, "Boy, that really stings."

I don't remember the exact day of my enlightenment, but I recall that I'd already decided I was a pretty good nymph-fisher.

It was on the South Platte on a nasty, overcast day (a good fishing day) when the water was the color of pewter and just as hard to see into. I set the hook for no apparent reason but with the absolute certainty that a trout had taken the fly. I wasn't at all surprised at the weight and wiggle at the other end. It didn't occur to me what had happened until I was holding the trout in my hands, and then I started to giggle. Sixteen inches, the best fish of the day; I didn't know how I'd caught her, and I didn't care, either.

I've heard dozens of other nymph-fishermen describe the same thing, and none of them has been able to explain it any better than I can. It sure feels good, though.

Ed still carries less gear and fewer flies than I do, and he still tends to take more fish, though I think the gap is closing. We've reached the point, however, where the competition between us (always friendly) has gotten very close to nonexistent. We hit the water now with a comfortable and familiar confidence that we'll catch fish and with the knowledge that the rivers, in their patient way, will put us down hard when we get too cocky. And when we meet, I do not bow from the waist and address him as "Master."

CHAPTER FOUR

The Bass Pond

I'VE HEARD IT CALLED "nervous water," a term borrowed from saltwater fly-fishers and applied, with less than complete accuracy I'm told, to warm, fresh water. A few nights ago A. K. referred to it as "electric." It's that thing a bass pond does in the late afternoon/early evening of a quiet, hot summer day when the fishing is about to get absolutely fabulous.

The pond seems dead, the water as smooth as a freshly wiped table top. The little blips of the smallest panfish have all but ceased, the frogs are silent, few birds sing, the mud hens and big Canada geese are anchored in an apparent state of meditation, their webbed feet dangling below them like Spanish moss. The leaves of the willows and cottonwoods dangle, too. It's hot, and there isn't a breath of wind.

Thunderstorms wander around out on the flatlands, good ones, dark slate gray right down to the ground, dangerous with lightning. They're far enough out that the thunder is muffled to the point of being subliminal, giving the relative silence the quality of a drumroll. The sky to the west, towards the mountains, is brilliantly clear, just going from that postcard blue of midday to something richer. The light is beginning to slant and thicken as it slices through more and more atmosphere. In another half hour it will be of great interest to color photographers.

The pond in question is one of several old gravel quarries that are now, after many years of being left alone except by fishermen and bird watchers, almost unidentifiable as manmade. The mountains to the west make this obviously Colorado, but with slight changes in vegetation and topography, it could be almost anywhere. It is a generic bass and panfish pond, immediately recognizable as such to any fisherman, as is this *feeling.*

A muskrat appears, hauling a mouthful of green weeds — working late, as usual — but most of the daytime creatures seem finished with their chores. A red-winged blackbird lounges on a cattail stalk in the same way a farmer will sit on his tractor seat for a few minutes in the evening to look back at the field he's plowed, not because it was such a satisfying day, but just because it's over.

At times like this it's easy for me to get contemplative in a phony, greeting-card sort of way and begin to anthropomorphize wildly, turning a blackbird into a weary farmer when I know it's just a bird and he's just sitting there. That kind of easy, cheap shot is unavoidable, and I'd probably get hopelessly tangled up in it if it weren't for the very real business of fishing.

Have you ever noticed that in virtually all portraits of mothers with babies, the woman holds the child with its head to her left side? There's a reason for that. It's because the real mothers, the models, almost always do it in the unconscious knowledge that the sound of the mother's heart is calming and reassuring to the baby. Someone noted that phenomenon and went on (at great expense in time and effort, one assumes) to figure it out, thus graphing and charting one more of life's fine little mysteries to no one's apparent benefit.

There's also a sound, scientific reason why a fisherman knows when he's about to have a screaming evening of bass fishing — why we stop to look at the pond and A. K. says, "Son-of-a-bitch, this is electric, man, *eeeelectric*" and digs out his big black-and-yellow deer-hair popper. I don't know what the reason is, and I wish whoever is responsible for figuring these things out would stop it. Those of us who take fishing as seriously as it *can* be taken enjoy these occasional moments of mysterious certainty and would prefer to be left alone with some of our illusions.

Out in the marsh at the back of the pond the green stuff is getting greener and the light brown stuff takes on a golden cast as the sun declines. As we slog in there (a place where few spin-fishermen in tennis shoes go) the water feels cool and we no longer sweat from the slightest effort. It is wonderfully quiet. A black-crowned night heron gets up in front of us and his petulant honk is clearly heard. From somewhere out there on the plains comes the sharp bark of a small dog, though it could be a fox. In the years I've fished here, I have seen foxes.

There is still no objective reason to believe the fishing will be anything but typical, but we hurry to the place where we can each cast to plenty of water and still be within wisecracking range of one another. I notice that A. K. has picked up some goose quills and has stuck them in his hatband. They're not there in a place or at an angle designed to be fashionable. He's a flytier, and he'll take these feathers back to his shop and use them as the forked tails on stone-fly nymphs. Free is free; waste not, want not; etc. He's an Iowa farmer in spite of everything, as recognized through the eyes of an Illinois bumpkin. Maybe that's why we fish for bass and panfish while so many of our colleagues specialize in "the trouts," though we do go after them with fly rods.

There's no sign of the small fish now — the little bluegills, pumpkinseeds, rock bass, and crappies — and I can't help wondering if they know the bass are on the way. I've got to cut that out. They don't know anything in the way I mean it. In fact, the very best fishermen, the anonymous gurus of the sport, understand that fish are stupid, regardless of what they tell you.

The first heavy boil is out against a weed bed. There was no question that it would show, the only question was where. I'll brag a little about what I do next because, for once, it's the smart thing. Rather than cast all the way across the shallow channel to that boil, I just flip my bug about ten feet out in front of me, twitch it once, watch the wake approach, and set the hook smartly a second after it vanishes in a sucking boil. I'm onto a fish that I very nearly spooked, feeling more smug than a little bass like this would usually warrant. Such is fly-fishing: almost anything that happens can be a triumph when the proper logic is applied. I glance behind me to make sure Archie is watching. He is. The fish is a chubby little largemouth of about 10 inches who comes easily, trailing a string of dark olive crud behind the bug.

The fly I'm fishing is a Black Slider tied in a #6 stinger hook, a sedate pattern as bass bugs go. The head is spun black deer hair clipped to something like a bullet shape so that it swims rather than pops. The tails are four long, black saddle hackles, longer than seem practical for the stubby hook, but it doesn't matter because a bass will invariably hit the head of a bug. The tails dangle down in the water like . . . What? Legs? The tail of some outlandish coral-reef fish no largemouth bass has ever seen? Perhaps they trigger prehistoric racial memories of drowning baby pterodactyls.

With a few exceptions (like mice and frogs), bass bugs are not tied to imitate specific creatures, but to copy life in general. It's a folk-art response to what a largemouth bass actually is: a big, nasty, hungry, gape-jawed fish whose typical feeding opportunities are almost too numerous to list. When compared to a cold trout stream, a healthy bass pond is as rich as a jungle, a stew of life so thick you can almost walk on it by midsummer, and a successful largemouth bass will eat anything that isn't big enough to eat him first. He's smart enough, or just belligerent enough, to nail something he's never seen before, as long as it looks alive and, therefore, edible. Enter the bass bug.

The little Black Slider is considered to be a "natural" big —
some would call it a Snakey — but it's too fat to be a snake, too
thin and the wrong color to be a frog, too long and thin to be
even a bullfrog tadpole, nowhere near a grasshopper or moth,
and so on. It's nothing in particular, everything in general — a
nondescript living thing struggling on the smooth surface of the
pond: helpless, vulnerable, food.

In recent years my bass bug selection has leveled off to the
Black Slider, a deer-hair frog that's rather plain and
impressionistic by current standards, buggy hair poppers in
natural (brown and tan), as well as yellow and white, yellow and
black, and the classic red and white. I also carry some big
Arbogast weedless Fly Rod Hula poppers, as well as the
inevitable late-winter-night-at-the-fly-vise-with-a-shot-of-whiskey-
one-of-a-kind-never-to-be-duplicated experiments that usually
vanish in snags, rot away on the hatband, or, rarely, actually
entice a fish.

The bright, gaudy bugs are required pieces of bass tackle,
heavy with tradition and light on rationale. It's been proven
experimentally that bass like certain bright colors, something
that's been known all along by bass-fishers, though as far as I
know neither the scientists nor the good old boys can tell you
why. The only thing that's clear is there's nothing in nature with
a pure white body, bright red head, and 3-inch-long tails. Such
things work, though, and exactly why will probably remain an
abiding mystery, like the fact that there are always bigger fish in
the pond than the ones you catch.

The more natural bugs, the sliders and frogs, are the ones I use
most often because they're the least outrageous, the closest to
real creatures, though the frog looks about as much like a *real*
frog as some of Picasso's nudes look like a person, and the
slider, as I've mentioned, doesn't look much like anything. But at
least it's black and not bright red.

With the first little bass landed, I'm false casting and working

out line. Maybe I should cover more water, but now I'm
thinking of that impressive-looking boil across the channel and
so, without further thought, cast to the far bank where the fish
last showed.

The bug hits the water (blat) more or less where I wanted it to
and I think, okay, I'm a big moth, or maybe a nestling blackbird;
I've just fallen into the water and, from shock and surprise, I
twitch once (incidentally straightening the leader). Then I wait,
helpless, puzzled. I wait for an indeterminate time, which is not
long enough, so I count to twenty-five and then twitch again.
Gently.

Having an instinctive belief that mental telepathy should work
on fish, I try to telegraph fear — I'm a helpless little bird who
has fallen into the water, what shall I do!? — but I can't help but
picture the lethal hook and so the message is impure, with an
evil laugh in it.

From the corner of my eye I catch a bulge along a floating
weed bed off to my right, and then I hear the whip, splash, as A.
K. hooks a fish. In spite of my supposed concentration, I turn to
look; Archie grins, and I flash my eyes back to my own bug in a
panic. But there was no strike.

Another boil farther out but still in reach, a different fish,
smaller.

I twitch the bug again, as faintly as possible, thinking, I am
growing weaker, I am struggling the wrong way, away from
shore. Then, after no more than ten seconds, I twitch it again,
harder. I tell myself this is tactical, varying the spacing and
strength of the jerks to be irregular and lifelike, but it's actually
eagerness creeping in. Be cool. Remember, fishermen are patient.
Picture the big bass down there watching the bug, backpaddling
with his pectoral fins, eyes leveled, waiting for whatever the hell
it is they wait for before they strike. But it's ruined. The illusion
dissolves. I'm too excited and there are too many other fish
working.

When the bass along the weed bed shows again, I pick the fly up and, changing direction without a corrective false cast, drop the bug a little too far from the edge. But it's okay. Before the leader is straightened, I can see the wake as the fish turns from the weeds and heads for the fly. The muscles of my arm tighten prematurely, but I wait until the fly goes down in the boil, set the hook smartly, and hear one of A.K.'s joyous profanities by way of congratulation.

Another 10-inch bass, and too easy even at that, but it tends to relax me some.

I shouldn't toss off 10-inch bass like that. Here in Colorado that's a decent fish on a fly rod, a keeper if you keep them, and therefore respectable. In the modest ponds where I do most of my bass bugging, you can count on a fair number each season between 12 and 14 inches, with the occasional fine fish up to 3 or even 4 pounds in daylight and maybe some even bigger if you go out at night a few times. That puts you in a class — sizewise if not numberswise — with the rubber-worm and live-minnow types.

In other words, this is not prime bass country, but it is bass country nonetheless. It's all here: the ponds with their quietly seething, complicated food chains, the sullen midday heat lifting into comfortable, fishable evenings, the heavy rods, goofy flies, short brutal fights, inexplicable dead spells, old-timers who watch the moon and stars — all the moody, fitful weirdness of bass fishing.

The fish are on now, charging and boiling along the weed beds and in open water. Who knows what they're taking? Little bluegills, damselfly nymphs? It's not a question you try to answer like you would on a trout stream, just a matter of idle curiosity.

When the bug is cast in the proper relationship to a prowling fish, it draws immediate attention. Some of the strikes are quick and instinctive, while others seem more considered, coming after a twitch and a long rest. We try to pick out the bigger swirls but are sometimes mistaken. Casting to what I think is a good bass, I hook a fish who feels odd on the line. It turns out to be a pumpkinseed big enough to cover my hand, a lovely, fat panfish who is large enough not to be intimidated by the bass.

Interesting. Possibly useful. Do the biggest old panfish feed with the bass because they have nothing left to fear from them? The thought is filed for future reference, though it's not likely I'll ever pass up bass to hunt bluegills.

We've taken a dozen bass between us, including a few relative rod benders, hooked and lost some in the weeds, and missed a few strikes. When it's like this I always feel that something beyond my clear comprehension is going on, though from a simpler perspective all that's happening is that the fish are biting, as they say.

Then it slows down, or rather, we *realize* it has slowed down, as a handful of casts each go unnoticed by fish. I glance over at A. K., who is changing flies. He shrugs. Changing flies seems like a good idea, although neither of us believes it to be the answer. It's more like one for the road.

I switch to one of my frogs, a clipped deer-hair job that's white on the bottom, mottled green, yellow, and black on top. These are not all that easy for me to tie, and it now and then strikes me that all the fancy stuff is on top where the bass never see it. An all-white body would work as well, be quicker and easier to tie, and would be more visible, to boot. It would not, however, be nearly as cute, nor would it look as snazzy hanging from the hatband.

Fifteen minutes pass. A.K. lands one more fish, and I miss a halfhearted strike, somehow getting a face full of line and a frog stuck in my sleeve in the process. A great horned owl comes in over the pond on huge, set wings and lands in a nearby bare tree. After stretching and preening for a few minutes, he settles into an ominous, predatory stillness, watching and listening for dinner or, in his case, breakfast.

A. K. utters the single word "beer" and we head out through the cattail bog, each step raising the familiar, warm, composty smell of the working marsh. A. K. passes right under the tree with the owl in it but, walking quietly and being too big to eat, he is ignored.

We meet on the dry, firm north bank and fall into a slow conversation: the fish, the weather, the owl, the flies. We've had many talks like this during which our eyes don't meet because we are both instinctively watching the water. As soon as cold beer is mentioned again we will walk for the truck, but it's not mentioned because we don't quite want to leave yet.

A. K. fills his pipe and I, for no other reason than that I'm standing at a body of water, cast my bug out and let it sit. More talk.

We're watching the place where the fly landed, but the light has all but failed and we've lost it. The pond has become a purplish disk with little detail.

I give the bug a good, hard jerk, and from directly below it the wake of a very large bass begins, heading away from us towards the deep water, obviously terrified.

A. K. and I look at each other then, eyes wide with surprise. It's not clear which of us starts laughing first.

CHAPTER FIVE

Fishing Commandos

THE FIRST TIME I HEARD about them was in a magazine article entitled, "Love Affair with a Donut." There are those who now call them "personal floatation devices." Just lately I heard them referred to as rubber duckies, and a friend calls his the *S. S. Fish*, two examples of that self-deprecating cuteness we fly-fishermen sometimes employ. I call mine a belly boat — the commonly used term and plenty cute enough — or a float tube.

I don't know exactly when they appeared, but the idea, like most ideas, is ancient. No doubt people were paddling around in inner tubes the day after the modern rubber tire was invented, though it took a while for some inventive angler to add a cover with a seat, a backrest (which holds a smaller tube and doubles as a backup floatation chamber safety device), a casting apron, and pockets for gear.

When I first became aware of them, my reaction was one of wise amusement: another ridiculous, useless, expensive gadget.

One either wades or fishes from a boat, period. I've since changed my mind about everything but their ridiculous appearance. Have you ever seen a grown fisherman waddling towards the shore of a lake with flippers on his feet, a personal floatation device around his middle, and a silly grin on his face? We all wear silly grins because we know how we look.

I came to belly boating slowly and cautiously, something I do more and more these days and which may be a sign that advancing age is beginning to diminish my inclination towards new thrills. In fact, it was that fear that finally got me into a belly boat, that and the fact that they'd been around long enough that few people would actually point at you and laugh anymore. I still didn't have a serious fascination with them, but they amounted to a new development that had survived the fad stage and I was beginning to feel left out.

Belly boats do have certain obvious advantages over wading or fishing from shore, all of which come under the heading of extended range. The first time I belly boated a pond I'd previously fished only by wading, I experienced an incredible feeling of power. I could fish wherever I wanted to (close in, far out) and could explore. I found offshore structures that I hadn't known about, caught fish from places that weren't even places to me before. It was as if I could cast like Lefty Kreh without having to take lessons and practice; it was, in fact, one of those rare times when the purchase of a piece of equipment actually did net me more fish.

I could have done all that from a boat, of course, except that there are two things about that particular pond that rule out real craft. First, it's a little farther from the road than I'd care to tote a canoe and, second, boats are illegal.

Boats are prohibited, but not *belly boats* which, on this particular water, are considered to be wading safety devices. Apparently, some confusion about just what a belly boat is is not uncommon, confusion that allows one to float on waters where he couldn't float before, at least for a while. We'll be able to enjoy this the way we enjoy the explosion of big fish in a new impoundment, knowing that sooner or later it will level off to something less spectacular. The bureaucracy will eventually catch up to us and put regulations on these things, if for no other reason than that they're fun and must, therefore, be illegal.

On the pond I mentioned (one of a whole bunch of ponds, actually) belly boats are clearly legal, at least until the man who's responsible for policing them is replaced by someone who is not a hot bass fisherman. On another lake nearby, where boats are allowed, some friends were recently told they had to sport boat registrations on their float tubes. On still another lake, administered by still another agency, things remain murky. The regulations read, "no boating or rafting," but, being aware of the vagaries of definition, I decided to check. The lake (reservoir, I should say) is owned by the local water board and the water board man said, "Right, no boating or rafting."

"Does that include belly boats?" I asked.

"Well," he said carefully, "no, I'm not sure that includes belly boats, that is, to my knowledge."

"So, you'd say that belly boats are allowed?"

"No, what I'd say is that I don't care to offer a legal opinion on the matter."

I don't know why this gentleman is wasting his time on the water board. His calling is clearly in law, politics, or philosophy. My mistake was in telling him I was the outdoor columnist for the local newspaper. I do that sometimes (it's true, by the way) simply in order to get accurate information. But in this case I blew it. If I'd just been a regular old fisherman (also true), the guy would probably have said, "Hell, I don't know, go ahead if you want to."

So I'm belly boating the thing — usually at night during the week when the competition from other anglers is slight and when the legality of the act is less likely to come into question. He didn't say I could, but he didn't say I couldn't, either. Right?

It feels a little like poaching and, God help me, there's a

certain thrill to that. I haven't felt quite the same excitement on landing a bass since I grew up, went straight, and got respectable. It's unlikely that I'll actually get busted because the regulations are so unclear, but if I do get hauled in, my defense is already prepared: a belly boat is clearly a wading device because, in a real boat, your butt is *not* hanging in the water.

Legal questions aside, a belly boat remains eminently portable in a way that even the lightest and smallest canoes aren't. I've never weighed my float tube, but I'd guess it to be 5 or 6 pounds, lighter than the daypack I carry. Granted, it's bulky and a bit clumsy, but still less so than a canoe. I never carried the thing twice the same way until Dale Darling (skipper of the *S. S. Fish*) showed me how. You simply place it on your back with the backrest sitting on the top of your head. Perfect. Both hands are free to carry rod and flippers, and the backpack goes in the hole in the tube. You look somewhat otherworldly looming out of the dark landscape after a day of bass fishing — dogs and small children stare wide-eyed and then commence to bark or cry, as the case may be — and your neck can get a little stiff after a few miles. Both minor problems.

The other disadvantages are largely psychological and can be overcome. I, for one, am not much of a swimmer, though I spend more time than most in and around water. Even after some experience, there's a feeling of vulnerability in a belly boat. You're hanging, butt down, legs extended, in an inner tube, over water of indeterminate depth. The first few times out I had not yet come to trust my craft and was a little nervous. It didn't seem to help to consider that this truck tube would support something weighing several tons. It still seemed fragile.

I thought I might get tangled in weeds and cringed every time something brushed the back of my thighs, a ticklish spot anyway, and there were darker fears, too. I was moving backwards and considered the possibility that I would ram the bow of the craft — which also happens to be the stern of the angler — into some hidden, sharp object. I also developed certain curiosities about snapping turtles. Would they be upset by my intrusion into their territory? What would they do about it?

Luckily my only two minor mishaps happened after I'd gotten used to the thing, so they didn't scare me out of the water permanently. The first was a genuine equipment failure. The plastic clip that holds the seat to the tube simply broke, dropping the seat and the pilot into the lake. It was startling, but I learned that you can't fall out of a belly boat — your elbows catch you. I replaced the clip with a length of nylon shoelace. It was a field patch that I planned to repair completely later, but when later came I realized that the clip had broken though the lace hadn't. And anyway, a good, workable patch is a thing of beauty.

The second episode happened just a few weeks ago. I was paddling through a weed bed on a favorite bass pond when I got tangled in something. I'll admit that I panicked a bit at first, but when I realized it wasn't a snapping turtle the size of a manhole cover, I settled down to assess the situation. At first, it seemed as though I was tangled in the weeds, something I'd about convinced myself wasn't likely to happen. On closer inspection, it turned out I was caught in a seemingly endless length of 20-pound-test monofilament, presumably with a big, evil, barbed hook on the open-water end. In theory, it was a simple matter of digging out the pocket knife and cutting myself loose, but in reality it took a good fifteen minutes. Belly boats are not designed to allow the captain to easily reach his ankles.

My personal rules for belly-boating safety are as follows: On general principles, I won't belly boat alone. This means that someone I know and trust must at least be on the bank. I have violated this rule only once when I was meeting someone on the pond and arrived early. What was I supposed to do, cast from shore when I knew the bass were in deep water? It went okay, but I was glad to see A. K. come loping up the trail with a no-nonsense, going-fishing stride. I said I was glad to see him, though he probably didn't take that the way I meant it.

I will also not belly boat in rough seas, though I'm now convinced that, with your behind below the water line, you're probably more stable than in any small boat. I just don't like waves breaking in my lap. And because a belly boat is not very streamlined, it's hard to make much headway against a wind.

I try to stay unencumbered by leaving the vest in the truck and carrying the fly boxes in one of the two side pockets on the float tube. The other pocket holds a canteen and some lunch.

One real problem is that belly boats are cold. Except in bathtub-warm, midsummer bass ponds, a creeping chill comes over you, making you want to get out and warm up, even though getting out is a chore and warming up steals valuable fishing time. In colder waters, the ones in which pike and trout live, you can get into a hypothermic situation way too quickly for my taste. You'd think the paddling would keep you warm, but it doesn't. It's not that kind of exercise. The solution to this is simple. You go out and buy a pair of neoprene waders and an equally expensive set of underwear and matching booties. The whole rig can cost about twice what you payed for the belly boat, but such is the nature of commitment.

I just recently spent the money after several seasons of belly boating over bass only, but feeling a gnawing sense of loss on trout lakes, where previously I had had no such feeling. The wallet gets lighter, the backpack gets heavier, and so it goes.

So far I've resisted getting a pair of the fancier and more expensive flippers that are turned up at the toes, making it easier to walk. I walk as little as possible in flippers now, usually just the few steps, backwards, down to the water.

New flippers remain a real, if faint, possibility, but I'll draw the line at a depth finder or one of those new belly boat outboards (water otters, I think they're called). At some point you have to either break down and buy a boat or learn to live with things the way they are.

The one thing I'd like to see on a belly boat is a workable pilot's relief tube. Dave Hughes, in his fine book *An Angler's*

Astoria, has warned us all to remember to pee before we put our waders on, but time still takes its toll. After having felt the call in a float tube, it's never again seemed like much of a problem while wearing regular old chest waders.

The manufacturers will send you detailed instructions on how to assemble and inflate belly boats, but I've never heard any good advice as to how to get in and out of them gracefully. The flippers get in the way when you're mounting up — whether you do it on land or in knee-deep water — and unless you're on something smooth, hard, and gently sloping, like a boat ramp, you'll feel like a beached whale trying to get out. What you want to do is paddle over to shore and simply step off, like you were hopping from your yacht onto the dock without spilling a drop of your diet cola. So far I haven't managed it and have, in fact, put several holes in my stocking-foot waders crawling up banks like a shipwrecked sailor.

That reminds me of another disadvantage. A leak in the waders, even a small one down at the ankle, will sooner or later put you in water right up to your waist because you are sitting in, not standing in, the lake. That familiar cold grip crawls inexorably up one leg, puddles under your seat for a while, and then begins the painfully slow journey down the other leg. The suspense can be unbearable.

When things are going right, as sometimes happens, the shortcomings of belly boats dissolve. You've managed to launch the thing without hurting yourself or providing too much amusement for the inevitable audience, and suddenly there you are, self-contained, mobile, able to maneuver with both hands constantly free. Experiencing the secret dream of every wading angler, you step off the drop-off shelf and paddle towards that delicious-looking sandbar 150 yards out. You're going backwards, of course, but you get used to that.

I've come to trust my boat now and feel harmonious when I'm in it. I'm set low to the water with something like a duck's perspective of things and have more than once paddled quietly within grabbing distance of fish, something you'll hardly ever do while wading. There's no telling what fish think of belly boats but, viewed from below, they must look enough like a cross between a goose and a turtle to seem like they belong there.

You've got mobility, silence, stealth, a low profile; it's a peaceful and, once you're in the water, at least, a graceful way to fish, though in a slightly different mood you could feel downright menacing. It's the belly-boat experience that resulted in a locally famous T-shirt slogan: "Fishing Commandos — Death from Above."

CHAPTER SIX

Camp Coffee

I USE A COMMON
American brand of coffee that you can get in big, three-pound
cans. It can be found on the shelves of stores, large and small,
throughout the West. On road trips I carry a pound of it. In my
backpack I carry some in a four-ounce tin that once contained
tea grown in India and packaged in England. It's enough for
several days out and the tin fits neatly inside the coffeepot. The
pot, in turn, goes in a heavy plastic bag to keep carbon smudges
off my clothes and other gear. Tidy, efficient.

A few years ago I experimented with some exotic — and
expensive — kinds of coffee for fish-camping but found them
unacceptable for a number of reasons. For one thing, the cost
was prohibitive. Not long ago I spent three-hundred dollars on a
fly rod, but an extra seventy-five cents for a pound of coffee still
rubs me the wrong way. Once established, priorities must be
maintained.

There was also the extra care and attention that brewing up a pot of some strange blend required in the field. The coffeepot is the hook from which a good, comfortable, homey camp hangs, but it should be as thoughtless as a rusty nail, not a big production.

And then there were the aesthetics of the situation. My gear, with some notable exceptions at both ends of the scale, is largely of moderate quality — serviceable, but not extravagant — and my camps are cozy, but far from posh. Espresso seemed out of place.

For me, coffee has always had at least a hint of the woods and rivers about it because I started drinking the stuff on fishing trips at what many would consider a too-tender age. I had my first cup in the kitchen of my Aunt Dora and Uncle Leonard's farmhouse before dawn on the morning of a bass fishing trip — or maybe it was a pheasant hunt. That's not the part I remember so well. What I recall is the oilcloth on the table, the straightbacked wooden chairs, Agnes the pet raccoon scratching at the back door, the whole no-nonsense atmosphere of the familiar, working Midwestern farm kitchen, the darkness outside the windows, and the morning chill. The cold is what makes me think it might have been pheasant season.

Bass or pheasants, it doesn't matter. I remember the coffee, in a chipped, heavy, well-used cup, as one of the early rites of manhood. There were others that have not served me as well.

That first cup (and many thereafter) was brewed by Aunt Dora. Though I payed no attention to the brand or the method used, I've judged all coffee since then by that standard, in the same way I've judged my own conduct in the field, and that of others, by the relaxed, competent, unhurried, droll example set by Uncle Leonard.

I especially remember the teen-age years when things like girls and fast cars were more on my mind than shotguns and fishing rods, but when fishing and hunting became what they remain for me today — a way out of, a way back from, a world that's faster, more complicated, and more ruthless than it needs to be

— there was always a pot of coffee simmering in the coals of the campfire or nuzzling around in the mysterious depths of a thermos bottle.

Between then and now I've consumed many more cups of coffee in civilized settings than out in the woods, but the aroma of the stuff is so inexorably tied to flushing birds, rising trout, giggling loons, drifting woodsmoke, and so on that they cannot be separated, even when the cup is made of styrofoam.

There was a time when I carried instant coffee in the field for the sake of speed and convenience. It worked for a while. In those days I was some younger and more eager for the kill. Drives, hikes, camps — they were nothing but means to an end. I was very businesslike and something of a guerrilla. Now that I think about it, I was also wet, cold, hungry, and/or lost more often than I am now and not as successful. I was in the process of proving something then that has now, apparently, been proven and forgotten. Going through a stage, they call it.

I think I started brewing real coffee in camp about the same time I began releasing all but a brace of trout because they're best fresh and because two is enough. "Enough" is a useful concept for the sportsman, especially the young one. I used the small aluminum percolator that saw me through college, when my main goals in life were to mess up my brains, get girls, and overthrow the government, not necessarily in that order. It did an adequate job.

It took A. K. to teach me how to make real camp coffee: bring one pot of lake or river water to a rolling boil, add two palmfuls of generic coffee, and remove the pot to the edge of the coals. If it's the breakfast pot, throw in the eggshells. When it's done (five to ten minutes), add a splash of cold water to settle the grounds.

Like whiskey, it should be drunk from a tin cup.

A. K.'s coffeepot goes back a long way. It sat on the banks of trout streams in Michigan for many years before it came to the Rocky Mountains and is now in its third stage of its evolution as

a camp utensil. First it was clean and enameled in some color
that is now lost to memory. Then it got all black and stayed that
way for a long time. Now the accumulated black gunk is flaking
off, exposing the battleship gray of the bare metal. Someday the
bottom will drop out and an era will have ended.

A. K. and I have drunk from this pot around countless fires
across several western states, but it has now become almost
synonymous with winter trout fishing in Cheesman Canyon.
That's a stretch of the South Platte River, one of those tailwaters
that stays open and more or less fishable throughout the year.
It's famous water and almost too crowded to fish in the summer,
but still nice and lonely on most days between Christmas and,
say, the end of March.

We've built coffee fires in several spots, but there's one place
that has seen the majority of them. It's where trout are often
rising to sparse midge hatches — slow, hard, technical fishing.
Sometimes we'll take turns on a pod of risers, one guy tending
the fire, sipping coffee, the other casting and slowly freezing in
the cold water. It was there that I hooked and landed my one-
and-only good-sized trout on a #28 fly and 8x tippet.

We use dead, dry willow twigs, and it recently occurred to me
that the few of us who build fires there have been inadvertently
pruning the little bankside brush patch, keeping it healthy
enough to provide the modest amounts of firewood we need — a
delicate and accidental balance.

A few years ago I made a comment in a magazine article about
A. K.'s bankside boiled coffee, something to the effect that it
was okay when you were cold and wet but that if you got a cup
of it in a cafe — too strong, with pine needles and nymph
shucks floating in it — you'd refuse to pay.

It wasn't more than a few weeks after the article appeared that
we ended up in the Canyon again. It was February, cold,
blustery, bitter, with drifts of snow right down to the water.
Sensitive to the early signs of hypothermia, I had left the river
when I began to shiver a little and headed upstream towards the

slightly bluish curl of smoke that told me A. K. had the coffee on. I rummaged through my pack for my tin coffee cup, finding that, amazingly, I'd left it at home. A. K. was delighted, saying it didn't matter anyway, since the coffee was no good. There was a lot of good-natured hell to pay before I could get my hands on his cup, all of which I deserved. Best damned cup of coffee I ever had, strong and black.

I can drink good coffee black, but I prefer it with cream. In a full camp I use real milk, but when working from a pack I vacillate between evaporated milk and that powdered, "non-dairy creamer." The powdered stuff is the most efficient, but I remain suspicious of it.

Coffee is okay on warm mornings when the wool shirt is shed while the bacon sizzles, but it's best on cold, winter trout streams, or during claustrophobic storms when the almost painful sting of its heat telegraphed through the thin walls of a tin cup seems like the center of the universe, a very real element of basic survival.

My first wife used a sterile-looking glass pot — more of a carafe, actually — and the coffee dripped with agonizing slowness through paper filters. It was always cold before it was ready to drink. My second wife used a tall, elegant electric percolator with a spout as long and graceful as the neck of a Canada goose. The noise it made while working was vaguely industrial. Once she gave up coffee entirely in the belief that it wasn't healthy. Of course it's not healthy; what is anymore? As Aunt Dora used to say, "Everything I like is either illegal, immoral, or fattening."

The coffeepot I've carried and camped with for more seasons than I've kept track of is of the old style: sturdy, heavy, enameled in the classic midnight blue under specks of white that are now fire-singed to a mellow brown around the slowly growing black patch under the spout — midway through evolutionary stage two. I bought it for pocket change at a yard sale and discarded the guts as soon as I got it home. It has been rinsed thousands of times but has never really been "washed."

Once I drop-kicked it twenty yards across a mountain meadow in Colorado (for reasons I won't go into here). When I retrieved it, the mineral deposits that had built up inside it rattled out like flakes of shale. The small dent it bears from that incident still shames me sometimes. Uncle Leonard would never have kicked the coffeepot.

For years that pot reposed with the rest of my camping gear and was brought out, along with sleeping bags, waders, fly rods, shotguns, etc., for what amounted to special occasions. Now it sits proudly on the stove in the kitchen as a symbol of freedom and simplicity. Why would anyone need more than one coffeepot?

At home I use tap water, but otherwise the coffee is made the same way as in the field. The glass knob in the lid of the pot disappeared long ago (in that meadow, maybe?), and just glancing into the kitchen I can tell the coffee is ready by the curl of steam coming from the hole it left.

CHAPTER SEVEN

No-See-Ums

THE RIVER IS DOWN,
fifty cubic feet per second, you guess, not really knowing but
trying to sound and feel authoritative. Your partner agrees,
"Yup, about fifty." Anyway, it's low and clear and the trout are
working. They're suspended, flashing lazily a foot or so off the
bottom. In the half of the river that's in sunlight, the water is so
transparent it seems unreal, exposing the trout. On the shady
side the current looks slow and oily. There are no rises or boils.

This is going to be tough.

Dropping the daypack and rigging up, you are exhilarated. It's
crisp, still, sunny, almost shirt-sleeve weather. You can see the
trout, and in the periphery of your consciousness you notice also
that the canyon is lovely — dark green and frosty looking on the
far bank with considerable snow under a sky that's cloudless and
bluer than on a feed-store calender. The month is February.

You want to catch these fish badly. They are rainbows, mostly,
the prettiest you know of, bright, strong, healthy, well-fed fish. It

will be a while yet before they spawn, but their reddish orange stripes are already taking on the neon quality of the annual sexual madness. No, not madness; let's say "preoccupation." These fish are too perversely mechanical and selective for true craziness.

So, you're exhilarated, but behind it is a faint feeling of bull-in-a-china-shop clumsiness. This is going to be a son-of-a-bitch.

Your partner's daughter, the photographer, is along on this trip for a working day off. Picking her up at dawn at her apartment near the university was the only hitch in the usual system that normally gets you out of town, heading south, in minutes. She was awake and ready, having seen Dad leave on countless fishing trips without even five seconds of lollygagging. She also looks very good, and you notice there is an element of mild paranoia in observing, even to yourself, that your best friend's young daughter is rather sexy. But it's only *mild* paranoia, an automatic reflex from a fading, misspent youth. The foulest profanities were deleted from the conversation, but otherwise the drive to the river was normal.

At a place known as the Channels, you rig up slowly, studying the situation. The trout are feeding steadily, which is good, but the water is low and clear, which is bad. The fish will spook easily. The currents here are braided, with the fish holding in spots that make long, downstream drifts highly problematic. This is also bad. Success will hinge on intangibles, like confidence.

Your partner wades in at the top of a long current tongue, moving to a spot where he's upstream of a Volkswagen-sized boulder. He's read it like you have. From there he can fish fine and far off, as they say, running his long leader down to where a pod of fish remains unaware of him for the moment. By his cast you can tell that the leader is unweighted, so he's fishing at the surface, probably with a midge pupa, assuming that, as the water warms, the hatch will thicken and the fish will rise. Maybe. Looking into the slanting light, you can see a few small midge flies sparkling in the air.

You wade out into the Channels, going carefully because the water here can go from ankle to armpit depth in a single step. You find the spot where the channel divides around a boulder shaped like a splitting mall. It fans to the right but plunges left into a pool (only about three feet deep now) that holds a pod of good-sized fish. They're in sunlight, throwing shadows on the bottom, and have not yet seen you.

With your hand on the midge box, several things strike you at once: it might *not* be the midge pupae; it might in fact be the Blue-winged Olive nymph, and if it *is* the midge, it could be any one of an inordinate number of patterns.

Changing patterns and sizes is a ritual of midge-fishing here. The trout are what we like to call "educated"; that is, they are well trained by heavy fly-fishing pressure and years of catch-and-release regulations to be careful what they eat. They are sometimes moved by the finest of distinctions, like a slightly lighter or darker shade of tan, a turn less of hackle, a pinch more of dubbing, a gold rib instead of silver. Actual pattern seems no more important than style and execution. I was once told the quill body of a certain midge pupa should be "a slightly muddy, brownish, medium-dark olive." Thanks, I'll work on it.

Looking into the midge box, you see a friend's pattern that has worked before. The body is a cream moose-mane hair, dyed olive, wrapped as a quill, with a head of tightly dubbed hares mask with a pinch of olive and a pinch of rust blended in. The friend was once asked a stupid question about that fly. "Is that dyed moose mane?"

"No," the friend answered solemnly, "that's natural olive moose. Damned rare."

It also strikes you that the pretty photographer is standing on the bank watching you, waiting for you to hook a fish before the light gets too flat and uninteresting. Light. The unavoidable, confidence-deflating thought is that at four o'clock the sun will drop below the other rim of the canyon, leaving the water in dun-colored shade. The trout will rise then and you'll probably catch some. That will be six and one-half hours from now.

The fly you choose is a South Platte Brassy. This is nothing more than fine copper wire wrapped, in this case, on a size 22 hook, with a turn or two of thin, charcoal-colored ostrich herl at the head. The herl for these comes from a ratty old feather duster, the good stuff from the fly shops being *too* good. It's a nondescript, marginal attractor pattern named for the river you're on, so it seems appropriate.

You consider not adding lead to the leader because it will likely spook the fish, but the fly has to get down. The trout are two feet from the surface, feeding casually, and will not rise. About 18 inches up the leader from the fly you put four turns of a Twist-on, a flat lead strip roughly the size and shape of a paper match. This you have soaked in vinegar to take the shine off. You've seen trout spook at the sight of shiny, new Twist-ons in this water before, especially on bright days like this.

All this fly choosing and rigging up wouldn't seem like it takes a long time except that you're being watched by a lady with a telephoto lens. For some reason, you can't quite get that out of your mind.

You flip the weighted rig upstream into what you think is the line of current that will slip it into the middle of the pool, but it swings wide. The next cast goes in closer, and the drift seems right. To keep the shadow of the rod off the water, you're running the fly downcurrent on a slack line. The only indication of a strike will be visual — a darting fish body or the winking gape of a white mouth. A short-line drift, with the rod tip directly over the weight, would be as disastrous as an upstream cast. You couldn't spook the fish any more completely if you waded through the pool.

You have what you think is the right drift now, but after five repetitions the pool is empty. You could see a few less fish with each drift, the larger ones going first, and though you never saw them leave, they are definitely gone. You feel a peculiar weakness in the ankles, the first sign of confidence washing away. Some days you just can't catch them, and this could be one of those days, with a photographer along to record it all for posterity.

You know what can come next if you're not careful. Once you've decided you won't catch them until evening comes and things perhaps get easier, you begin to fish automatically, doing it by the book but without that tense, predatory spark that makes it work. You'll change flies without the light of intuition, your backcast will begin to drop, and you'll eventually execute the dreaded self-fulfilling prophecy.

You begin to work upstream, looking for another spot. It would be nice to find some fish working in faster water, but that's unlikely. The water is too cold for the trout to want to expend those calories; your legs ache from it a little through the waders. The midges are also too thin for fast-water feeding. No, they'll be in the slicks and slow pools. The photographer is nowhere in sight. She's probably gone up into the rocks to find some of those pretty, miniature landscapes with moss and a twisted ponderosa pine.

You work upstream, spooking three more pools with three different flies, finally coming to the place where the river is a single channel again. Here it runs shallow and sandy to the left but deep and green along rocks to the right. Some trout are lined up there in no more than two feet of water, below and to the side of the heavier current, just up on the slope of the sandbar. One looks rather good, 16 inches, maybe; it's hard to tell.

You've been spooking fish, so an evaluation of how close your patterns are to what the fish want is nearly impossible. Still, there's the dim hint that it could be the Blue-winged Olive nymph you considered in the beginning. It's a common bug here, making up a large part of the insect population, so common it has been known to work in all kinds of situations. You change to a #20 Pheasant Tail nymph (a little too big to be the midge pupa, about a size small for the *Baetis* nymph). There is the flavor of intuition in this.

You approach your casting position in a half crawl, half duck

walk, settling on your knees still 6 or 8 feet from as close as you
could get. You are telling yourself now that the key to low-water
midging on a calm, bright, sunny day is to somehow enter this
crystal-clear, completely exposed environment without disturbing
it. This seems possible; you have forgotten that you can't catch
these fish.

The cast will come from almost still water. It will have to
hook upstream into the edge of the current. The fly will sink and
tumble down behind the weight on a slack line, tightening in the
vicinity of the trout while the tip of the line stays more or less in
one place, turning downstream as the fly passes.

You make a side-arm cast, to keep the shadow off the water,
and the gentle blip of lead striking water just inside the current
seems in about the right place. There is movement from the fish
then, but he hasn't spooked. Did he flinch at the cast, or did he
just happen to eat a bug right then? These tame trout don't
necessarily vanish when spooked, but they can get into a state of
mind where they might just as well have.

You imagine where the fly is, downstream from where it
landed, moving slower than the current, still on a slack leader
but coming up on the swing. The trout makes another little
move, like the first; without thinking, you've set the hook and
he's there.

You and the trout are equally surprised at this tight line
between you. There's an instant when neither of you makes a
move, but then he's downstream, through the riffle, and boring
in the pool beyond while you are still down on one knee.

You stand and follow him; he runs to the back of the pool,
pulling line from the reel, but then stops. The run gets shorter.
It's a beautiful, clear, sunny day. You can hear the quietly
breathing rush of the water and the early spring song of a water
ouzel, but beyond that is silence, not even the click of a camera
shutter.

CHAPTER EIGHT

The Fly Collection

I GUESS I HAD A
collection of flies long before I was aware of the fact. Whenever
I'd get to poking around in my gear looking for something else,
I'd come across a fly that I'd stashed for some reason or other.
Maybe it was a beautiful example of a Red Quill from a friend
or a streamer tied by a favorite guide. Maybe it was just a fly I'd
never seen or heard of before or since — as good a reason as any
to save something. Some were given to me as examples of
obscure tying techniques or regional pattern preferences, others I
was supposed to fish but didn't because they were too pretty. A
few were examples of local patterns from here and there that I'd
saved for "future reference," whatever that means. A few were
authenticated with business cards or even letters from the tiers;
most were not, but in all but a few cases, I could remember
where they came from.

They turned up in the kinds of odd places where you put
things you've planned to save for no clear reason, and I suppose

I became an actual collector the day I got together as many as I could find and tossed them all into the same drawer.

Since then I've approached the collecting of flies a little more seriously; that is, I've started to *think* of myself as a collector — still with no clear reason.

I have a few pieces now that might be worth something (a pair of lovely dry flies by Walt Dette, for instance), but that's not my main focus. Every collector, myself included, would love to have museum-quality stuff — flies by the great modern and historical tiers — but, although I'm always on the lookout for something fabulous, a more modest approach fits my temperament and finances much better.

Only a few of the flies in my collection cost me more than the going rate for commercial ties, and most of those came from fund-raising auctions where a few drinks, the heat of the moment, and a righteous cause turned my head. It's at these times that I get into the true collector's bind: on the one hand, no collector wants to pay as much as a thing is actually worth (if that can even be determined), but on the other hand, if you really lust after something, no price is too dear.

For the most part, though, the pieces in my modest collection are not what most would call "collector's items," but I'll hasten to add that a collector's item is anything I or any other collector says it is.

I don't specialize in any particular kind of fly, but I do have a weakness for more-or-less established patterns tied by their originators and one-of-a-kind or prototype flies. I have, for instance, several early variations of a now-standard local stone-fly pattern by Jeff Swedlund, as well as a downright weird thing of his that never quite caught on called a Hopper Popper (a complicated grasshopper fly with a bass-bug-style cupped cork head). I'm probably among a handful of people in the entire world who own a Hopper Popper tied by the originator — or by anyone else, for that matter.

I own a number of flies by A. K., who is well known for his

crisp dry flies. He tied Eastern-style flies in Michigan for years, but his style changed after he'd lived in the Rocky Mountain West for a while. His dry flies now have heavier tails and hackles, but somehow they retain that fine, delicate silhouette we associate with Eastern flies. If I needed a reason for holding on to some of these, that would be it, but to say something like, "these flies represent the meeting point of two fly-tying traditions" would probably amount to a load of pretentious crap. The flies are just neat, and I'm not a scholar.

It could be that my favorite A. K. Best fly is a huge and ugly, but immaculately tied, bass bug he whipped up for me a few years ago when I was on my way to a local bass pond. It could only be described as a kind of top-water, bass sculpin and he fully intended for me to fish it; he even turned down the barb, but it was too goofy and pretty to get wet. I mean, a *fish* might have chewed it up. It now sits on top of the gun case, clamped in the jaws of a retired vise, as a reminder that fishing should never be taken too seriously.

There are delicate dry flies by Dave Student and Bill Purdy; sturdy caddis flies by Dale Darling; tiny, buggy South Platte River midge pupae by Edison Engle; and a gorgeous full-dress Silver Ranger by Mahlon Ozmun, to name a few. Those names may be familiar to some of you; to most they're not, but I'd be willing to bet that at least one of them will be a household word in years to come, and their good early work will be worth something. In other words, though I don't have any flies by Theodore Gordon, maybe I have a few from the *next* Theodore Gordon. In any event, it's as close as I'll ever come.

Collectors always talk like that. Speculations about worth and value (two distinct things, by the way) are inevitable, even from someone who, just a few paragraphs back, claimed not to care about such things. Tom Finn, aside from having a great name for a fisherman (second only to Bill Trout), ties the cleanest, most perfect bass bugs I've ever seen. His clipped deer hair looks like cork. He'll probably be famous for them someday, and I've got some. If he doesn't get famous, I've got flies by a guy who no one has ever heard of but who smokes everyone they *have* heard of, which may be even better. Worth and value.

There are no flies in my collection that aren't, in my opinion, beautifully tied, and now and then I pull one of them out to use as a model. The fact is, though, that most of them have only sentimental value, which makes them worth much more to me than if they'd been tied by big names with whom I'd never shared a ride, a drink, a leaky tent, a smoky campfire, or whatever. If I live long enough or pass the collection on to the right person, it may someday turn out to have some monetary or even historical value, but I think I can honestly say that I don't care much one way or the other. I'm just having fun with it.

Professional tiers are well represented in my drawer, but easily half the flies are by dentists, carpenters, the editor of a well-known fishing magazine, a mechanic, a musician, various people whose professions I am unaware of because it's never come up, and some assorted trout bums — all folks who aren't professional tiers for reasons other than that their work isn't good enough. I bought some, traded my own flies or materials for others, and a few tiers simply gave me flies when I mentioned that I wanted something of theirs for a collection.

Last year I got a fly in the mail from Bob Damon, who now lives in Oregon but who, back in the 1920s, tied the pattern for his father and a gentleman named Charlie Gunning who fished on the St. Vrain River, the stream that flows past my front door. The fly was accompanied by a letter from Mr. Damon telling about the days when the St. Vrain held cutthroats instead of the browns you'll catch there now. I consider this one to be a local artifact of considerable significance, and I show it off every chance I get.

Before A. K. moved to Colorado his favorite river was Michigan's AuSable, and he has in his collection some flies by a man, now deceased, who fished that river regularly many years ago. There are a few recognizable patterns, but many seem to be experimental. My favorites are some huge dry flies that look like crosses between caddis flies and wolf spiders. Stuff like this is either worthless or priceless, depending on how you look at it.

There are many ways to approach fly collecting, only a few of which will cost you more than a few dollars here and there. If you get into full-dress Atlantic salmon flies, for instance, or authenticated flies by historical figures, you're looking at some heavy money, but on the reasonable side you can still assemble an interesting, even impressive, collection.

You might want to specialize in classic dry flies, realistic nymphs, streamers, or bass bugs. Maybe you could collect regional grasshopper patterns. You might even want to go about it the way I do and just pick up whatever turns you on at the moment.

My only stipulation now is that I know who the tier was, if that's at all possible. That's usually not a problem, but in a tray marked "so and so's flies," the pattern you pick up may be by the maestro himself or by one of his anonymous tiers. I usually don't care one way or the other; I just want to know.

Sure, maybe one of these guys will be famous some day and I'll have the flies and the documentation, but that's not really the way I look at it. Fly-tying, like any craft, approaches being an art form when it's done very well, and fine flies by any tier are worth enshrining for no other reason than that, at least for now.

More than once I've begun plans to display the collection in some way, but I never seem to get around to it. For that matter, I'm not sure things like this belong under glass as long as there are actually fish out there to be caught. They're more fun to paw through, handle, use as models for my own tying, or just produce some evening when the conversation drifts around to flies. The furthest I've ever gotten is to move them into a bigger drawer.

CHAPTER NINE

Kazan River Grayling

THE KAZAN RIVER IN Canada's Northwest Territories is a strange one, as rivers go. It rises in the interior at sprawling Snowbird Lake and eventually empties into Hudson Bay some 900 miles to the east, but up near the headwaters it's nothing more than a series of channels draining one lake into another. What is cavalierly referred to as The River is, in this area at least, largely a figment in the imagination of some cartographer. Its course, if you can call it that, is difficult to locate on a map and downright incomprehensible from a boat. It's worth finding, however, because these little stretches of river — some no more than a few hundred yards long and separated by hours on a hard boat seat — hold some world-class Arctic grayling.

There are grayling in most of the lakes too, usually in the shallow bays and coves and around points of land, but the largest ones in this particular part of the Northwest Territories are typically found in the stretches of fast water known collectively as the Kazan River. According to the guides, the grayling stay out of the deep water to avoid the enormous lake trout, and they shun the weedy backwaters for fear of the northern pike, or "jacks," as they're called.

Now that's a homespun theory attributing more thought to the fish than they're capable of, but I still like it, and the larger fish (those weighing in at between 2 and 3 pounds) *are* in the river. In fact, two fly-rod world-record grayling came from the Kazan. Both weighed just a hair over 3 pounds when caught and an ounce or two under by the time they were officially weighed. For comparison, the all-tackle world-record grayling — the largest specimen ever recorded — weighed in the neighborhood of 5 pounds, about the same as the world-record bluegill.

I was working out of a fishing camp on Snowbird Lake in the company of Wally Allen and, typically of both of us I suppose, we were clearly doing things backwards. The main attraction for most anglers in this remote area (130 miles by float plane from the nearest settlement, 275 miles from the nearest road) are the lake trout, or mackinaws. They're not called macks up there, though, probably because it would rhyme with jacks and cause a lot of confusion.

Whatever you call them, fish in the 30-pound class aren't uncommon, and that's what most people come for. The grayling aren't exactly looked down upon, but they tend to be viewed as something to amuse the sports when the lake trout are off or when they've become jaded from taking too many huge fish on ¾-ounce jigs and T-60 Flatfish. My friend and I, however, had come loaded with fly tackle mainly in pursuit of grayling and so were considered by the camp staff and guides to be harmless, though definitely odd.

The Kazan rises near the southern end of the 70-mile-long lake, about a twenty-minute boat ride from the camp. There's a half mile of brawling, marginally navigable river before you come to the next lake, which remains nameless on the best local map. This is the only part of the Kazan that anyone from the camp

had ever felt moved to fish, and it's a fine piece of water with
pools, glides, pocket water, riffles, and one set of genuine
standing-wave rapids. It's just like a real river except that it
begins and ends too abruptly.

This is the stretch we fished for the first few days, heading out
across Dehoux Bay towards the river while the other guides and
sports — some flashing us puzzled expressions — motored out to
fish the submerged glacial eskers for the Big Fish. We had it to
ourselves for a few days, but it wasn't long before we began to
pick up some company.

During the inevitable talk over supper at the camp, it came out
that we were taking some grayling that nudged current records.
(In my limited experience with guides, I've found that you can
bribe or beg them into just about anything except keeping quiet
about the big fish they've put their clients onto which, after all,
is fair enough — it's like asking a painter not to sign his work.)
An International Game Fish Association record book magically
appeared and was studied carefully by some of our colleagues,
who admitted that the lake-trout fishing had been a bit slow. As
Colorado fly-fishermen and, more recently, grayling specialists,
our mildly oddball status was revised to the tune of several
lukewarm Labatt's beers, and we were summarily pumped for
details.

Grayling are an exotic species of fish to most American
anglers. In appearance they fall somewhere between a trout and a
whitefish but are in their own class with that beautiful,
flamboyant dorsal fin used in mating displays. Whether they also
use it for navigation is, apparently, arguable, but I believe they
do — it *feels* like it when you have a good one on the line. I'll
admit that's less than a purely scientific observation, not unlike
assuming the fish live in the fast water to hide from the pike.

The color of an Arctic grayling is hard to describe and can
only be hinted at in color photographs. They're subtly iridescent
with hints of bronze, faint purple, and silver, depending on how
you turn them in the light. They have irregular black spots

towards the front of the body and light spots on the bluish
dorsal fin which, on many of the larger Kazan River fish, is
rimmed with a pink stripe at the top. They're so pretty, I never
quite got used to them.

In Latin they're known as *Thymallus arcticus* because they're
supposed to smell like thyme, though I can't say I ever noticed
that, even though I sniffed a few fish when no one was looking.
My olfactory memories of the trip are confined to pine,
mosquito repellent, and the fabulous aroma of shore lunch:
baked beans, homemade bread, onion rings, fresh fish breaded
lightly in cornmeal, and industrial-strength camp coffee.
Although the delicate white meat of the grayling is excellent, it
still comes in second to the pink-fleshed lake trout.

For the record, we used barbless hooks and released most of
our fish, as one is encouraged to do by the management of most
camps and by the Northwest Territories Wildlife Service, whose
conservation policies are very up to date though difficult to
enforce in a largely roadless area covering well over a million
square miles.

A phrase like "a million square miles" is like "a billion
dollars" — you know it's a hell of a lot, but beyond that, it's
meaningless. The poetry of the word "wilderness" makes a lot
more sense to me, and when I try to conceive of the incredible
size of the Northwest Territories (most of the water in which has
never been fished, by the way), what comes to mind is the cairn
of shed caribou antlers that stands on the beach in front of the
camp. This area is big enough and wild enough that herds of
these animals can migrate across relatively small pieces of it and
remain more or less ignorant of the existence of human beings
on the planet.

The Kazan River grayling behaved almost exactly like trout
except that they were much easier to lure up to dry flies (when
they weren't already rising) than any of the trout I've ever
personally known. In fact, dry flies were consistently more
effective than nymphs, even for the larger fish, and going under

water didn't move larger fish, as it often does on a trout stream.

They weren't exactly selective, but they weren't idiotic, either. Yellow Humpies and Elk Hair Caddises in sizes 16 and 18 worked consistently, but when we got too far from those two in either size or color, the action dropped off noticeably. The Kazan is largely a caddis river (we saw no caddis flies larger than a size 14, most smaller) with a liberal smattering of mayflies, midges, and even stone-flies, but the caddis seems to be the main food source. By the way, all aquatic insects are collectively referred to as "fish flies," as in "big brown fish fly" or "little yellow fish fly."

I can't remember when it was that we got the itch to explore more of the Kazan than just that first stretch. Maybe it was on the third or fourth day. That far north the days run together, literally as well as figuratively, with almost none of what you'd call "night" and sunrises and sunsets that would last for hours and almost run together. It was a little dreamlike at the time, and in hindsight it's close to hallucinatory.

Going down the Kazan was not the usual procedure; in fact, no one had ever wanted to do it before, and so there was some discussion about it. Eventually, the camp manager located some waterproof maps in the storeroom, suggested we make this our last beer, and told us we'd be going with a different guide in the morning.

After breakfast the next day we lugged our gear down to the beach and were greeted with, "I am Guy LaRoche, forse class Franch Cunadium feeshing guide; get in zee boat, eh?" The man was young, hard as nails, steely eyed, good on rivers, and all business. Terrific.

We crossed the bottom end of Snowbird, white-knuckled the short rapids in the first stretch of river, and set out across the nameless lake. It was bigger in reality than it looked on the map, was spattered with small islands, and had at least one pair of bald eagles nesting on its banks. We fished the channel at the bottom end and then set out across Obre Lake. Obre, dotted

with larger islands, was long and deep enough to land a float
plane on, and so it had a camp. We stopped, but it was deserted,
and in the middle of the season, too. Obviously the owners had
gone under. Running a fly-in wilderness camp is an expensive
proposition: I was told that by the time the gasoline for the
outboards was barged up to Stony Rapids and then flown into
the camp at Snowbird, it ended up costing between seven and
eight dollars a gallon. No figures were available for beer.

We spent something like a twenty-hour day (most of it riding
across lakes at full throttle) in order to fish three stretches of
river that, laid end to end, might have been two miles long. I
couldn't help thinking of that chapter in Richard Brautigan's
Trout Fishing in America in which he describes a hardware store
with hundred-yard sections of trout stream stacked out back and
of the fact that that book — one of the great pieces of modern
surrealism — has been innocently filed under "Fishing" in the
Longmont, Colorado public library.

The second channel down from Snowbird was long and wide
with an easily wadable shelf; it was big, slow water that called for
some long casts.

The next channel was a fast, deep rip of three or four hundred
yards that we located first by cruising the bottom end of the lake
until we found the spot where the weeds began to lean in the
imperceptible current and then by the sound of the white water.
It was a treacherous spot full of big grayling. We landed few
under 2 pounds and a fair number pushing 3. It was here that
Wally took one of the fish that would become a new fly-rod
world record, and it was at the bottom of this stretch that we
found the remains of what had once been a crude but very
serviceable wooden canoe and a hand-carved paddle — a chilling
find, especially so because a search was going on at that very
moment for a plane that had gone down somewhere in the area.
It was never found.

It was also in this stretch of fast water that I got myself into a
spot from which I had to be rescued. I'd hooked a lovely big

grayling about midway down the rip on a #16 dry fly and a light tippet. The fish jumped once and headed down into the fast current, peeling off line and starting on the backing, of which there suddenly didn't seem to be nearly enough. The bank was too steep and overgrown for me to get out and follow him, so without thinking, I started downstream and quickly waded into a scary spot that I couldn't wade back out of: I ended up at the top of the rapids in nearly chest-deep water, unable to move an inch towards shore and in the slow but steady process of being sucked into the white water (where I would have gotten a brutal dunking at best, and might easily have drowned).

As luck would have it, Wally came along about then. Assessing the situation immediately, he sprinted off through the trees to find the guide, who would have to interrupt his afternoon nap to, as it was told later in the guides' shack, "save the miserable hide of the dumb American."

I didn't know how he was going to handle it, but I was immensely relieved when I saw Guy push off from the bottom of the rapids and — first things first — swing out around my line so I wouldn't lose the fish. He motored up through what passed for a channel in the rapids, deftly flipped sideways (presenting me with a fast-moving gunwale at the level of my forehead), and yelled, "Get in zee boat!"

So, I got in zee boat, scattering rods and tackle boxes, and Guy, with absolutely no expression on his face, calmly handed me my fly rod. Out in the still water of the next lake I took up the slack, and the fish came out of 15 feet of water to make one more beautiful jump before I landed him, whopped him on the head with a knife butt, and tossed him in the cooler for lunch.

One of my clearest memories from that trip is that fish's last jump. Grayling are great jumpers, usually coming out of the water three or four times before they're played out, and they do it with fantastic grace and style. They actually *look* like the paintings of leaping fish you see on calendars — seeming to freeze for an instant in that perfect arc before diving cleanly back into the river.

While I was dealing with the fish, Guy was examining the outboard — seems he'd dinged the scag, that blade-shaped piece of metal that protects the prop. Actually, it was broken clean off, but guides never "break" anything, though they may "ding it up a little."

If he *had* wrecked the boat or motor, stranding us in the middle of nowhere, it would have been my fault, but he paid me the supreme compliment of not giving me a lecture, assuming that, although I was a jerk, I was at least smart enough to know it. A lot of information can be conveyed by a single blank look.

He did, however, stop off at a local shrine on the way back to the camp. It's a pair of graves set on a low hill overlooking the southern end of Snowbird Lake, the kind of place that's chosen not so much for the benefit of the deceased as for those who'll come to visit. No one knows who's buried there, maybe French trappers or some folks from the party of Samuel Herne who discovered and named the lake on his way to the Arctic Ocean. It's clear they've been there a long time, though: the inscriptions on the wooden crosses have long since weathered away. When the camp is opened in the spring, one of the first orders of business is to send someone over to clean off the graves and straighten the markers. The hill is near the place where the fish are cleaned, across a small bay from the camp, to keep the wolves at a respectful distance.

It wasn't as heavy-handed an object lesson as it might seem; every sport is taken there once during his trip, and we'd already had a good laugh by way of writing off the incident in the rapids as a harmless screw up. Still, there *was* something about the timing. I guess I should have felt lucky, or realized that perhaps I'd just blown my last chance for a truly glorious death — something few of us get a shot at anymore — but none of that occurred to me until later. At the time we were tired and happy, and Wally had a world-record grayling down in the cooler. It was a pretty spot, though, just a nice, peaceful place in the north woods.

CHAPTER   TEN

Cane Rods

I JUST SPENT THE
better part of a day moving my friend Paul's stuff into my
perpetually half-finished attic room, where it will reside at least
until next summer when he comes back from the Corkscrew
Swamp in Florida. I don't mind providing this service; it's the
dues I pay for being in my late 30s, single, with a place of my
own. Over the years here I've had the worldly possessions of
several friends piled in one corner or another and sometimes the
very friends themselves when they found themselves in those
unavoidable spaces between jobs, wives, and cheap places to live.
I consider it karma from having been on the move myself in the
past. I guess a man in my position necessarily runs a repository
for the gear of wandering buddies and a halfway house for
wayward husbands. It also helps that I live next to a trout stream
and am not likely to use the butt section of a flyrod to prop
open a window. Old reliable John.

During the course of this most recent of Paul's moves, I finally inherited Clyde. Clyde is the mounted head of a mule deer (with a modest rack) that was shot around here in the 1920s and who has since gazed glassy eyed from the walls of half the houses in the county. He's getting a little shopworn but is, after all, a local artifact.

With Clyde hung on the wall, Paul and I drank a toast to his trip, reviewed our plans to meet in Tampa in the spring for the cosmic bass fishing trip, and walked out to his vintage Volkswagen, a vehicle that will make it from Northern Colorado to Florida in the winter only by the grace of the gods.

The last thing he said to me was, "By the way, if anything weird happens, see that my folks get my stuff, but keep the Leonard." Then he got into his pitiful heap and drove away. Nice. The proper sentiment from a departing fishing partner delivered without embarrassment, speeches, or any unnecessary syrup at all. Very nicely done.

The Leonard in question is a lovely old 8-foot split cane, one of those rods that somehow didn't get used up in its youth and that comes on now as an agelessly beautiful and dignified, though still playful, older woman. When Paul got it we spent an afternoon out in the yard casting it with different lines, trying to decide which one it took. We settled on the double taper 7. I tried to buy the rod; Paul firmly, smilingly, declined the offer, and, as near as I can remember, I haven't seen it since. He left it here only because it's too light for where he's going.

Now I appreciate the gesture of friendship — even though neither one of us expects I'll collect on it — but what's interesting is the glimpse this episode presents of the inner workings of the cane-rod fanatic. Paul has a lot of stuff (I know, I've moved it all several times — the dues I pay for owning a pickup truck), but the only thing it occurred to him to make some arrangements for in case he got squashed on the road or eaten by an alligator was his best cane fly rod. Interesting. Revealing. When placed in a spot where he was forced into evaluating the meaning of all the things he owned, the fly rod floated immediately to the top, while the graphite rods remained, with the rest of his life's accumulations, under the broad heading of "my stuff."

Split-cane rods will do that; there's something about them.

I developed my own craving for bamboo rods during the last days when they were almost unanimously considered to be the best you could get — top drawer. For years the only real alternative had been fiberglass, a perfectly good, durable, workable, cheap material that still somehow lacked a certain hard-to-define mark of quality and prestige. Arnold Gingrich used cane rods, so did Charles Ritz. In early issues of *Fly Fisherman Magazine*, large trout were pictured lying on the banks of trout streams next to fine cane rods, though in recent years dead-fish-on-the-ground shots have gone out of fashion. Even back then (not all *that* long ago, after all) good cane rods by the better makers weren't cheap, although, looking back, I see I should have hocked everything to buy Leonards.

I bought my first cane rod, a Granger Victory, about the time that graphite had emerged from the rumor mill into the light of day. It wasn't something you just heard about anymore; you could go to some fly shops and see a few of the new rods on the rack. They were long, too skinny, too black. They looked fragile but deadly in the finest tradition of modern technology.

Many fly-fishers who saw themselves in the vanguard of the sport raved about them shamelessly. There were stories of the unexceptional fly-caster who picked up a gleaming new graphite stick and put a #2 weighted Muddler Minnow in the trees on the far side of the lake, ripping line and backing from the reel and nearly breaking his wrist in the process.

There were darker stories, too, of the new rods exploding on the first run of a 100-pound tarpon, filling the face and chest of the unsuspecting angler with shrapnel. Neither story was true, apparently.

Graphite was, and is, good stuff and it sold, though more than one eager fly-fisher was disappointed that he couldn't cast any

farther with his new space-age rod than he could with his old
Eagle Claw glass. Someone was heard to say, "Spend half of
what you just spent on that rod on some casting lessons, and
you'll get your extra distance." Those words were spoken by a
member of the old guard, a man who maintained a degree of
suspicion.

"Graphite? Like in pencils? Jeeze!"

Most of us switched to graphite, either immediately or
eventually, with or without reservations. A few stood staunchly
by split cane and fewer yet stayed with fiberglass. These last are
the true, unsung cranks of this story, though some of the fine
new glass rods make them look like prophets, now. They also
saved themselves a hell of a lot of money.

Split cane did not disappear, of course, any more than it did
when it was supposedly replaced by fiberglass in the 1950s.
There were even continuing tips of the hat in the marketing of
graphite rods: "It has the casting action of bamboo but with the
strength, sensitivity, and light weight of graphite." Okay, fine.
"Use this new toothpaste and you *will* get the girl." Remember,
this all takes place in America.

Incidentally, that advertising tactic has just recently come full
circle. The Orvis Company, speaking of their first new split-cane
design in a decade, says it has "a crispness that compares
favorably to our more delicate graphite models." Now that's
nothing more than intelligent marketing, and I'm sure it's a fine
rod. I just wonder if the comparison sounds ironic to anyone but
me.

In any case, the plastic rod has arrived and is now considered
the standard, the "state of the art," as they say in every other ad
you see. This came home to me last August when I went fishing
with a gentleman who was not only unimpressed that I was
carrying a split-cane rod, but was actually puzzled that I would
fish with such a thing. His own rod was of course made of
graphite, and I'll admit he threw a long, beautiful line with it.
Lovely to watch.

He was cautious and polite (one does not, after all, blithely insult another man's program to his face), but in the course of the day's fishing he trotted out all the stock arguments for graphite over cane: the newer material is lighter, stronger, more powerful, more sensitive, etc.

There was also some scientific-sounding talk. It seems to me that the emergence of graphite has turned many fly-fishers — formerly only amateur entomologists, icthyologists, and historians — into dabblers in physics as well. I heard about parabolic curves, stress coefficients, and other things that can make vague sense to me at the time but seem to dissolve later. In the past I've slipped into that kind of jargon myself when trying to speak authoritatively about fly rods, but I could never quite shake the feeling that, to someone who understood the concepts, I must sound like a thirteen-year-old boy discussing women.

I do, by the way, understand what a parabolic curve is because you can draw a simple picture of one: it's a line that bends more at one end than the other. As far as I can tell, *all* flyrods and most sticks exhibit parabolic curves when wiggled.

Even if I couldn't understand exactly what my friend was talking about, his message was clear: graphite is demonstrably better than split cane in all ways, even to being much cheaper and needing almost no special care. It is eminently practical.

My defense was basic and nontechnical: I've fished with cane rods for a long time now, and I just like them; they please me. There's the live heft and feel of real wood, the pleasant weight of them that tells you your back cast has loaded (making it unnecessary to glance over your shoulder), not to mention the baggage of tradition.

Moving the discussion from the technical to the emotional seems typical of cane-rod types. The question becomes not which kind of rod is the most practical but whether the concept of practicality has any place in fly-fishing. As Len Codella of the Thomas and Thomas Company once said, "If all we cared about was catching fish, we'd not only be fishing with graphite rods, we'd also be using worms.''

Cane-rod maker Mike Clark comes close to refusing to discuss the matter, even with a sympathetic soul like me. If you don't live in Northern Colorado, you may not have heard about Mike's rods, but you will.

You may also not have heard of G. E. Lipp cane fly rods. Gil Lipp has, sadly, gotten out of the business in favor of a better-paying career (and also, I suspect, in the interest of not turning something fun into a job), but he left behind a handful of gorgeous, crisp, tippy, darkly impregnated rods. I own two of them. One is a quick 7½-foot, 4 weight that Mike Clark told me, after caressing the thing with a micrometer and consulting his notes, is built on a Garrison taper. The other is a short 5 weight built on the Charles Ritz "parabolic" design, wherein the ferrule is set below the middle of the blank, making the butt section considerably shorter than the tips and making, also, for a very goofy-looking rod bag. The rod is "2 meters" long, a concession to modern terminology. For those of us who speak only English, it is about 6½ feet, give or take a millimeter.

Gil, who has a way of putting things concisely, once said that a fly rod is made of bamboo, period. Anything else is just a cheap, plastic imitation. He happened to say that while unknowingly in the company of Joe Fisher of the J. Kennedy Fisher Rod Company, makers of, you guessed it, graphite rods. There was a short, strained silence, after which the two men were introduced. Joe, sublimely unoffended, smiled and put out his hand, and Gil said, "Pleased ta meet ya, Mister Fisher," not giving an inch.

Even in bamboo-rod catalogs, where you might expect to find some quasi-technical justification for the use of split cane, you see only passing references to tradition, delicacy, and grace. That's because the people who write these things know they don't have to enter the debate. Maybe you're just used to the best of everything, maybe you've got a deep streak of nostalgia, or maybe you're someone who has reserved this one corner of your life for an expensive indulgence. Nothing matters except

that you're there on page 37 looking at the cane rods, for
reasons of your own.

Oddly enough, and speaking of catalogs, the cane-rod
aficionado of today has more ways to go than ever. For the
collector and/or maniac, there are the true museum pieces, rods
by the great makers like Leonard, Howells, Payne, Garrison,
Gillum, E. C. Powell, F. E. Thomas, Paul Young, and others.
These fine pieces are so expensive now that my interest in them
is only marginal. Oh, I'm impressed, and when I see one I look
long and hard. They are, after all, genuine artifacts of fly-fishing
history, as well as exquisite casting tools. Anymore, though, I
don't even want to see the price. I'll probably never own a
painting by Picasso or an automobile by Rolls Royce, either, so I
just don't ask.

Even if I did own an 8-foot, 5-weight Garrison (as long as
we're dreaming, let's *dream*) I'd be faced with the decision of
whether or not to fish it. On the one hand, it would be a thing
of true historical value, irreplaceable, the ownership of which
could translate into a responsibility to future generations of fly-
fishers. On the other hand, it would be a tool that was lovingly
and carefully crafted by an artisan of legendary skill for the sole
purpose of catching trout. It would likely have been used in that
way by several serious, discerning anglers before it came to me,
people whose spirits might become restless at the thought of
their favorite rod languishing in retirement.

Of the three people I know who own Paynes, one fishes his
rod regularly (to the point where it now needs to be refinished
for the second time), while the other two fish theirs on what
amounts to an occasional to *very* occasional basis. I guess you'd
have to take your Rolls Royce Silver Cloud out for a spin now
and then too — on dry, clear days, in thin traffic — though you
probably wouldn't haul your firewood in it.

Next come the rods by the modern makers, the big companies
like Thomas & Thomas, R. L. Winston, Orvis, and, until
recently, Leonard. These are all good rods. In fact, they may well

be among the best split-cane fly rods ever made, being the results of generations of knowledge and tradition coupled with modern tools, glues, and so on. New from the factory, they start at just over $500 and go on up to well into four figures, depending on all the things price depends on. The prices of new, top-of-the-line and custom rods overlap those of the collector's items by the old masters. If a guy had, say $1,200 to blow on a fly rod, he'd have an interesting decision before him. This is not something that keeps me awake nights.

Equal to these in range of quality and price are rods by the independent craftsmen around the country: Walt Carpenter, Ron Kusse, Bob Summers, Charlie Jenkins, Gary Soeffker, and my neighbor, Mike Clark, in Lyons, Colorado. There are others, some with more or less famous names, others known only to a handful of cane-rod freaks. A few make some sort of living building and restoring rods, while others work in the evenings and on weekends, producing a handful of rods in a year's time — doing something not for the profit so much as for the satisfaction. I called one of these gentlemen once to ask some questions, and he told me he'd write back but wouldn't call. "I'm just a poor rod builder," he said, "I don't initiate too many long-distance calls." He might have added ". . . to destitute trout bums who can't afford my rods anyway."

True enough, though the few handmade rods I own have been good to me. My Mike Clark rod was built more or less to my specifications (if you can call "a crisp, tippy, 8½-foot 5 weight" specifications) and it's right up there with the best rods I've ever cast. I fish it so often I sometimes have to force myself to use another rod, something I do more and more now, trying to postpone the day when I have to take it back to Mike for new guides and ferrules. A. K. was so impressed with it he got one like it, though not *just* like it. His is ever so slightly, just noticeably, slower.

This, it turns out, was intentional. Mike knew that I'm an admirer of that nebulous quality in fly rods known as "backbone," a preference that, in my case, may be symptomatic of inferior casting style compensated for by brute force. I know it's fashionable for fishing writers to deprecate their casting and other skills, the assumption being that we're actually quite good and also modest. But I'm not kidding. I'm a solidly mediocre caster, which is why I like to fish good rods; I figure I can use all the help I can get.

A. K., on the other hand, is a fine, stylish, unhurried, graceful caster who, thank God, also screws up now and then. He can get the most from a rod exactly like mine except that it flexes a hair slower and a little deeper into the butt. Regardless of what you hear, this is the meaning of the phrase "custom rod."

The G. E. Lipp 7½-footer has been used long and hard and has stayed straight. I'm waxing the ferrules now for a tighter fit and will probably have to get them replaced in another season, two if I ease up on it a little. The 6½-footer is a sweet little specialty rod that's reserved for hands-and-knees beaver-pond casting and tiny brook trout and cutthroat creeks. It may last forever.

The Mike Clark is one of his early rods, number three. His first six rods are all owned by local fanatics; they were snapped up when Mike finally emerged from his chilly, cluttered workshop, handed out business cards, and offered rods for sale.

The G. E. Lipps, aside from being fine rods, are deliciously enigmatic, two of only twenty ever produced, three of which have remained with the maker. "A G. E. what?" people say.

Most of the cane rods I've owned come under the heading of "used." They've turned up in strange as well as predictable places, including the used rod lists published by dealers like Thomas & Thomas, Martin Keane, Walt Carpenter, John Bradford, and others.

It's in this state of having been previously fished that many fine and otherwise out-of-reach rods become available to those of us with modest budgets. Just looking over a couple of more-or-less current rod lists, I find an R. L. Winston 8-footer for a

#5 line for $390, an Orvis 8-foot Battenkill for $240, a 5-weight Leonard for $295, and here's an 8½-foot 6-weight Garrison for only $2,650. You get the idea.

When you get into the Grangers, Heddons, Phillipsons, South Bends, and Shakespeares, you reach the magic figures (at this writing, at least) of $200 and under or, to put it in perspective, no more than, and sometimes less than, a new graphite rod. These are the rods that really interest me, the ones that are affordable enough to send me searching through the checkbook and peering ahead through the maze of bills, groceries, gas, and beer money for the next two months. These were the standard-production rods, the over-the-counter fishin' poles to several generations of regular old, garden-variety American fly-fishers. In this way, I find them even more romantic than the Paynes and Gillums.

The best of these rods are clearly the Grangers and Heddons. One cane-rod dealer told me the top models by these two makers are typically comparable in quality to the best fly rods ever made, with no exceptions mentioned. Top production models would be the Granger Registered and Premier rods and the Heddon Model #1000 and #50 Presidents. In the early 1950s, the Granger Registered and the Heddon #1000 both sold for $100, while the Premier or the President would set you back $75 — relative peanuts now, but not back then.

A. K. owns a Heddon President, refinished once by Bob Summers and again, recently, by John Bradford, and it's one of the sweetest, prettiest fly rods I've ever been allowed to cast. I didn't exactly offer to buy it, just asked him to call me if he ever thought of selling it. He glared at me almost angrily for an instant and then dissolved into peals of laughter. I don't see the rod that often. He only fishes it on special occasions, a special occasion being defined as any time the President is strung up, though the rod has never been bent by any creature but a trout.

Still, this top-of-the-line business, while useful, is also a little deceiving. I once lost a bidding war over a Heddon Black Beauty that was lovely to look at and cast, an excellent rod, even though in that same early '50s catalog, it was listed below seven more expensive, and supposedly better, models. My own Granger Favorite, exactly in the middle of the line, is the best 4 weight I've ever fished with, and my 8-foot, 5-weight Victory, the cheapest rod Granger made, is a little darling.

The Phillipsons are also fine rods, with the Premiums and Paramounts at the top of the list. These rods were a continuation of the Granger tradition. Bill Phillipson worked for Granger until 1946, when Granger was acquired by the Wright & McGill Company, when the Phillipson Rod Company came into being, and when I was born, not realizing that I would someday be lusting after fine cane fly rods that were, even then, being made in Denver, Colorado.

Phillipson aficionados typically rave about the power of these rods, which were designed, after all, for windy, Western fly-fishing. One of the Phillipson models was actually called the Powr Pakt, an early example of that trend in American advertising that has resulted in a whole generation who sincerely believes that quick is spelled "kwik."

Some of the South Bend and Shakespeare rods are fine, serviceable, middle-of-the-road rods — many still in use — though most of their cheaper models are real clubs. The rods by Bristol, Montague, Horrocks-Ibbottson, and a few other makers of downright cheap fly rods are typically, as Gil once said, "as worthless now as they were the day they were made."

Then there are the exceptions. A. K. once dug up a wonderful old rod, long and light, with excellent cane work, a swelled butt with rosewood inserts, fancy wraps, the whole ball of wax. John Bradford, who seems to know as much about old rods as anyone in the business, identified it as a Montague. A Montague? According to John, the rod makers at the Montague Company would, now and then, break down and build a gorgeous rod, as a special-order, presentation model, or just to prove to themselves that they could still do it.

Exceptions. Many of the "hardware-store rods," produced by any number of production rod makers for various retail outlets, are of relatively poor quality, while others, bearing names like Abercrombie & Fitch, Spaulding, and others, are of appropriate quality. Many of the best of these rods are Heddons, though it takes a trained eye to tell.

This is where I should point out that I'm far from an expert on cane fly rods. I think I can spot good ones and appreciate them when I get my hands on them, but that's about as far as it goes. A real expert reading this chapter will likely cringe at the omission of some names. So be it. You don't have to be smart to be in love.

The rod lists I get in the mail are constantly revealing the names of rod makers (good ones, judging by the prices) of which I wasn't aware. D. J. Duck is a recent example. Even my favorite rods, the Grangers, continue to surprise me. Just when I thought I had them down to the Registered, Premier, DeLuxe, Favorite, Aristocrat, Special, and Victory, I stumbled on a pretty, red-wrapped, "Denver Special." Not long after that, along came a "Streamer Special." And so it goes.

I thought I had the Phillipsons down, too, until I heard about the "Haywood Zephyr," the only Phillipson model I've heard of that doesn't start with the letter P. It's worth noting that the most expensive Phillipson was the Premium, while the cheapest model was the Paragon, either of which sounds like it should be the top of the line. That sort of thing is common with production cane rods and it's worth watching out for. As far as I know, no one in the history of fishing tackle has had the nerve to offer a "Not Too Bad" or "Works in a Pinch" or "Better than Nothing" model, though that's what some of them were.

The good, reasonably priced production rods surely won't last. I bought my first Granger over a decade ago for $50. Not bad. The same rod today in the same condition should sell for around $200, and that's not the kind of thing that's likely to stop or turn around. There are still some screaming deals

around, but the days when fine production cane rods turned up
at flea markets marked "old fish pole — ten bucks" are all but
gone. You're more likely to find a crooked Montague with short
tips going for $100 because "that's one of them bamboo fly
rods; they're *valuable.*"

Even with sniffing out bargains, the cane-rod madness can get
you into some financial trouble. Most of my fishable cane rods
cost me less than $200 each (well, okay, let's say not much *over*
$200), but I traded a fairly valuable rifle for my R. L. Winston
and paid dearly for my little Thomas & Thomas Special
Trouter. I bought that T & T new, off the rack, because I came
to realize I couldn't live without it and because I don't see many
used Thomas & Thomas rods. People seem to hang on to them.
The little 7-foot Leonard I had for a while didn't come cheap
either, and the guy I sold it to had to go on the installment plan
to buy it from me.

I referred to "fishable" rods earlier. Not long ago I traded for
a 6-weight Heddon that was sound but far from fishable.
Everything was there, but the ferrules were loose, the varnish
was cracked, and some of the wraps were coming undone. It was
together enough that I could cast it on the grass and come to
realize I had to have it, but it would have broken down in a
week of hard use. Partly by pointing out that it would need a
complete refinishing job, I got it for a relative song.

It's now down in Fort Worth, Texas in the capable hands of
John Bradford, getting a complete facelift. When I talked to
John about it over the phone, he asked, "Do you have much in
this rod?"

"Not much," I admitted.

"Good," he said, "because it'll be worth about what you're
going to pay to have it restored."

That's fine with me. What I traded for was raw material.
What I'll end up with is about a $250 fly rod that will be every
bit as good as one that could easily cost me two or three times
that much and that will be, in addition, a bit of a collector's

item. I might have gotten the work done a little cheaper, but that's exactly what I'd have ended up with: a little cheaper job. I've seen a lot of these vintage production rods come back from John's shop looking every bit as good as they did when they were brand new, often a little bit better in the varnish department. Any rod that's worth restoring is worth sending to a top pro in the business.

"A couple hundred dollars for a *fishing pole!?*" You'll hear that all the time if you don't keep your mouth shut in certain company. You can talk about the aesthetics and even mention that a cane rod will appreciate in value while a new graphite rod will *de*preciate, but the best thing to do is turn around and say, "$9,000 for a *car*? I only paid $500 for mine."

I like to fish with good cane rods and I manage to do it without suffering too much in other areas of life. Still, I have the sinking feeling that in a few years a guy won't be able to do this unless he's rich or even crazier than I am. Feelings like that (and my suspicion that the last really good pickup truck went out of production fifteen years ago) may be nothing more than signs of growing older. If that's the case, then Carly Simon was right when she said, "*These* are the good old days."

I don't mean to give the impression that I have a massive collection here. At the moment, in the room that serves as a "den," there are about a dozen cane fly rods from 3 to 7 weight, heavy on the 4s and 5s. The two thunder-stick rods, an 8 weight and a 9 weight, as well as the little-bitty 2 weight, are, yes, graphite. But the spinning rod (a Phillipson), the bait-casting rod (a Union Hardware), and the two ice-fishing rods (homemade from old, unidentified tip sections), are all split cane. So there.

It's not massive but I suppose it *is* a collection, if only because there are more rods in this house than a sane man needs, but then "need" is as vague a concept in fly-fishing as "practicality." The fact is, I'm casually in the market for a long, 8-weight cane bass rod, still looking for a Heddon President I can afford, while at the same time the house could use some work, the truck is running a little rough, and my clothes remain just on the respectable side of ragged.

I called Gil a while ago to ask, for the record, just how many rods he'd made. I was sitting here at home with my feet on the desk and he was, I'm sure, in about the same posture down at his office where he makes good money but — sadly, as I've said — no longer builds flyrods.

They're still much on his mind, however, and I should say that he's mellowed considerably on the subject, allowing that a guy can fish with a telescoping tubular-steel fly rod if that's what turns him on, and he'll get no argument from Gil Lipp. He has also spoken glowingly of some of the new glass rods he's seen, but I know for a fact he still fishes mostly with short, light split-cane fly rods of his own making, a unique and enviable distinction, even among purists.

I told him that in this chapter I had evaded the technical arguments between cane and graphite and he thought that was wise, offering as the only justification he could think of the fact that fly-fishing is a sport in which fish are caught properly only in a certain way, often against all odds, and that using rods made from a weird kind of grass that grows in China seems somehow appropriate.

CHAPTER ELEVEN

The Fisher of Small Streams

THE FISHER OF SMALL streams can come home tired, maybe with sore knees or a bunged elbow for a souvenir. He will have covered some ground. Back at home he might feel a little old, especially if it's an early trip taken while his physical edge is still dull from the winter, but then he'll remember how far he went, all the pretty brook trout, and he'll feel like a kid. That night he'll probably sleep like a kid, too, drifting off on the comforting wings of egotism — a man with, he tells himself, an aptitude for rugged country, honestly bushed.

Where I live, in the eastern foothills of the northern Colorado Rockies, there's an incredible diversity of fishing. In the reservoirs and farm ponds on the plains, you can fish for bass and a full complement of panfish, as well as the odd walleye and some perch. In some of the higher reservoirs, you'll find northern pike, a fly-rod quarry which doesn't get a lot of attention in print but which will rattle your teeth and bite your thumb off if he can. A respectable game fish.

There are some lake trout (mackinaws), which I have, at this writing, yet to capture on a fly here in my home state, and there are the real trouts: browns, rainbows, brookies, and cutthroats. Up north are two of the few places in Colorado where you catch grayling. Over on the Western Slope are some good whitefish streams. There's one alpine cirque lake containing golden trout and grayling; you can typically catch the latter there but not the former.

There are kokanee salmon here and there, as well as white bass and "wipers," the white bass and striped bass hybrid.

You can find places where every species comes bigger, but there aren't a lot where you can take them all in at least respectable size within day-trip or overnight range of home. Much of this is within a hour's drive of my house, and the house itself sits across the street from the catch-and-release stretch of the St. Vrain River (St. Vrain *Creek* on some maps) — brown trout water.

I don't consider myself lucky because my location wasn't a matter of luck. To be honest, it wasn't exactly planned, either. It's just that when I was out West looking around after college, I realized where I was and was smart enough to stay. Whatever else one can or can't do around here, he can pick his fishing the way a connoisseur picks wine from a well-stocked cellar. Let's see . . . what kind of mood am I in today?

Over the past several seasons, I have set myself the task of exploring the many small mountain streams in the neighborhood: the fine blue lines that connect the dots on the topographic maps of the area (the dots are the lakes). Many of these little creeks are anywhere from underfished to ignored. They're dabbled in some where they flow under roads or past campgrounds, and some of the larger ones are fished well up towards their headwaters, but mile after mile of them is simply left alone. The inevitable fisherman's trail peters out within a mile or so of the access point. They're often on steep grades, making them fast and white, and although they're pretty in a nonangling sense, they seem to come under the heading of "babbling brook" rather than "trout stream" in the minds of most fishermen. There may be trout, they think, but they'll be too small to fool with.

In some cases they're right, but (there's always a "but" in fly-fishing, isn't there?) in spots these little creeks widen and deepen in response to some wrinkle in the topography, and there you can sometimes find good trout water and good trout. One thing we have plenty of here in the Rocky Mountains is wrinkles, and it doesn't take much of a pool to grow a handful of fat, keeper-sized brookies or cutthroats.

Some of these spots are obvious to anyone who studies maps. The thin, blue line of a creek appears up where the tight contour lines show the Continental Divide. (The map won't show the clusters of tiny snowmelt feeders that would look, if they were there, like the shallow roots of a weed.) It flows roughly east or west, depending on which side of the Divide it's on, pointing towards one ocean or the other. Sooner or later it comes to a place where the contour lines widen. The line on the map that represents the creek stays the same (remember that cartographers are concerned with the course of a stream more than with its nature), but in your mind you can see the water sprawl out and the current slow. You can almost hear that incessant babbling muffled.

A little piece of a map like that can haunt you, especially if it's in an area you frequent. You've seen the stream where it crosses the road, and it's not that great looking. You've also seen it five or six miles up, where it leaves the lake. Pretty small and spartan there. But there are those miles in between which contain, the map tells you, a little meadow. And, although the map shows only that blue line with no variation in size and no feeders, you can see there's a hell of a lot more water down low than up high.

You know that six miles in this country can be a momentous bushwhack. You know also that a little flat shelf on a map does

not necessarily mean a stretch of deep, slow meadow stream
with undercut banks that hide big trout, but you know it *could*
mean that. The farther off the beaten path it is, the better. Only
a maniac would hike miles of steep, brushy stream to fish that
one good hundred-yard run. That's the point.

Then one morning you wake up feeling daring and with either
a free schedule or the guts and the inclination to play hookey.
You take a light rod, one fly box, hip boots, a canteen of water,
and a substantial lunch. If someone happens to be around, you
mention that you're going fishing — which is completely obvious
and no surprise to anyone you know — but you don't mention
where. The possibility exists that you'll want to keep this very
quiet.

More often than not, I end up having myself a nice, long, hard
walk in lovely country with no company, on which I manage to
hook and land a handful of small trout. That's not bad in its
own right. Now and again, though, it will pan out.

I know of a short series of stair-step pools — tubs — where
one finds four-foot-deep water on a stream otherwise sadly
lacking in good trout habitat. There's a single, big-bend pool
against a rock ledge that is deep and mysterious and that
remains in shadow for all but an hour or two of every day. The
riffle at its head pumps in a steady supply of bugs, while the
slow, shady water encourages the fish to feed. They're rainbows
and cutt/bows, no more than a foot long at best, but deep
bellied, bright, and healthy. They're the kind of trout which,
when photographed carefully with no rods, hands, or pine cones
in the frame to show the scale, could easily pass for two
pounders.

The prettiest spot I can think of offhand is on a little three-
mile stretch of creek that connects two high lakes. It's close to
the top lake but is down in an alternately rocky and brushy little
canyon that all the smart fishermen go around because the
walking is easier on the higher ground. It's in a spot where the
lay of the land seems likely to produce nothing but a shallow,

fast little piece of water. Because the lake itself is quite good, it took me several trips there before I decided to try the stream. Flowing out of the bottom end of the lake and off through the trees, it touched either my sense of adventure or my wild-eyed greed. It was, after all, *more* water that might hold *more* good fish.

The chance I took was a gamble, but a well-considered one. I left the lake in midafternoon with a feeling in my stomach not unlike hunger, brought about by the suspicion that I was walking away from a cosmic evening rise. It took courage. I figured to slog down the stream, achieving the lower lake by nightfall. The truck was parked not far from there in a spot I could find in the dark if I had to. I figured there would be a rise at the inlet down there, if nothing else. The lower lake holds only modest- to small-sized brookies, while the upper one has respectable cutts, but it would be better than nothing.

Where the stream left the lake it was all but hidden in mats of nose-high willows, the kind of terrain that always reminds me of the New England farmer giving directions to the city slicker: "Well, young feller, you can't get there from here." It was trout habitat, though — structure, shade, almost bassy looking — so I fed a little wet fly down in front of me, taking a brace of finger-long cutts before I bagged it and just walked.

The falls were exactly where a fisherman would have put them: well out of sight and sound of the lake, separated by nearly impassable brush, but not too far away, maybe a half mile. At first I thought I was hearing the wind in the spruce trees (it sounded just like that), but there *was* no wind. The hair stood up on the back of my neck.

Above the falls was a fifty-yard-long flat, fairly deep, with bubbly current coming in at the top and an absolutely glass-smooth flow dropping out the back. The only indication of the falls from that angle was the sound and the occasional errant drops of spray that looked like caddis flies in the sun. Two or three fish rose at the head of the run, with a few more coming up at the tail.

It would be too much to ask that these trout had never seen a fly or leader before, but I doubt they'd seen many. I crept and crawled and cast so carefully, but when the #14 Adams landed on the water at the inlet — too far to the right and a little too far back — the largest trout I could see swam over, looked at the thing long and hard, and then swallowed it with such innocent confidence it would have broken the heart of a more sensitive fisherman. He fought hard but not smartly, and came to the hand with an air of astonishment. He was a plump 15 inches, his size clearly the result of that "eat anything" attitude of his.

The second fish from the same spot was an inch shorter, but otherwise a twin of the first. Two more at the outlet, and the pool was spooked.

They were all cutthroats with light-olive backs, shading to yellowish olive sides spattered lightly with large, round spots of an absolute, interstellar black. The slashes on their jaws were orange instead of red, as were the almost irridescent gill covers. They were short and stubby for their weight, the platonic ideal of the high-mountain cutt, unquestionably perfect in every way, even to being stupid.

It took twenty minutes of scrambling through boulders and brush to get to the bottom of the falls, a distance of maybe twelve feet from the top. The water sluiced out of the pool above over a polished rock shelf, then dropped off an overhang into a beaver-pond-sized pool. The rock face was covered with brilliant-green glistening moss, watered constantly by the spray. The pool itself had the blackish olive color of depth under the falls, shading out into a reddish brown rock bottom towards the outlet. It looked like one of those Chinese watercolors except that the sun was shining. If you happened on the place in a fog, it wouldn't seem unreasonable to meet an ancient oriental gentleman painting lines of poetry on willow leaves and sailing them down the current. I was out of breath from the climb down, but it wasn't only that that made me just stand and look for what seemed like a long time.

A few small trout rose here and there at the tail of the current, but I kept watching the hole. It was of a depth you seldom see in this type of country except in the lakes. You could have hidden a car in there, or an enormous cutthroat.

But there was no big cutt, or at least I didn't hook one, though I tried a weighted nymph and then a big, black Woolly Bugger streamer, a thing large cutthroats have been known to eat. The only trout I took were small, a few cutts and one lonesome brookie. So this was the boundary. The trout up above must be lake fish who had wandered down the current to find the one spot where they could live easy and grow fat. Did they come down as fingerlings or as adult trout? Did they ever go back to the lake? Did they even *remember* the lake? Idle curiosity. What mattered was that they were there, rising in the same bright sunlight that had put down their relatives up in the lake, stream fish now, however they came to be there.

The walk out was hard. I whacked the bushes for half the distance but, finding no interesting water on the stream and seeing the light fade, I took to the hillside, which was more open but steep and crumbly. I reached the inlet of the lower lake at dusk, stopped for a few minutes to admire the brook trout rising there, and headed for the truck, wondering if the last of the coffee in the thermos was still warm.

Thinking of those willows reminds me of another creek. This one flows for miles through what at first glance looks like a parklike meadow but which is, in fact, a hellish tangle of grown-together willows, wide channels, bogs, sinkholes, and decaying beaver dams. It contains the entire list of types of terrain you don't want to have to walk through, but the fishing is pretty good.

It was up this creek a few years ago that I gave up the use of those stretchy cords for my landing nets. I was alone, a mile or so up in there, hip boots sucking in the thick mud, arms and fly rod tangled in the brush, face scratched, sweating, mosquito bitten, and a little discouraged by the fact that I couldn't seem to find the stream. Couldn't even hear it.

That tugging I felt at the back of my neck turned out to be the landing net, which had tangled in the willows, pulling the elastic cord tight to a length of about four feet. When it came loose, the base of the wooden net handle cracked me hard in the base of my skull. As my brain began to go black, I could picture the headlines: "Local Angler Killed by His Own Net — 'A Case of Incredible Clumsiness and Stupidity,' Says Coroner."

I came just short of losing consciousness, spent a short time being quietly stunned, then commenced to howl, curse, cry, and otherwise carry on, finally coming to several realizations at once: I wasn't seriously hurt, wasn't too badly embarrassed (there being no witnesses), wasn't stuck as badly as I first thought, wasn't going to die, and actually did have a fair idea where the stream was. It's funny how quickly things can clear up with a slight change in attitude. I finally found the water and managed to catch a few trout, none of which were big enough to require the net.

The fact is, you seldom do need a net on these little streams. The fish are rather small, but there are two ways of looking at that. They may be little in the grand scheme of things, but they may also be exactly as big as they're supposed to be in small, fast, steep, broken water with a short growing season. When you spot a nice 8- or 9-incher finning in a little slick behind a rock in a diminutive creek, he looks to be about the right size.

Around here he'll likely be a brookie, cutthroat, rainbow, or the ubiquitous hybrid of the last two. In a few places, some at surprisingly high altitudes, he may be a brown. Whatever he is, he'll be bright, sleek, and wild, not indigenous, but definitely a homegrown fish. He'll be one of the descendants of stocked or planted fish from the lakes or larger streams who have wandered off by themselves to live a harsh but largely undisturbed life. If you kill him and eat him, he'll be pink fleshed and succulent.

I like a short, 4-weight rod for small streams, preferably split cane, and I usually fish a weight-forward line to get the weight out quickly for short casts. My two favorites are a Thomas & Thomas and a G. E. Lipp, both in 7½-foot length, though last year I started using a little 3-weight cane built on a Sharps blank. I'm told Sharps doesn't *make* a 3-weight blank, but they either made this one or it's not really a Sharps. I have only the word of the guy I bought it from. Wherever it came from, it's an elegant little rod with a slow action that goes right down to the corks. It does justice to a 10-, 8-, or 7-inch trout and will hold one much larger if you keep your wits about you.

Get yourself a light rod, fish the small streams until you're used to the scale of things, and then hook a 12- or 14-inch brook trout or a 15-inch cutt. Sooner or later it will happen. That fish will be breathtakingly large. You may panic and break him off.

I can guarantee that unless you happen to be a victim of the Big-Fish Syndrome. That's a disease that affects people who have a mild character flaw anyway and who then fish Bristol Bay, the Big Horn, or some other water where the landing of countless fish over 20 inches (that mystical number) "ruins" all lesser fishing for them. Don't laugh; I've actually heard people claim that. When I was a boy in the Midwest, the same condition was known as "The Mopus," in which the sufferer became filled with crap right up to his heart.

Though all fishermen have a thing for big trout, most are immune to the more virulent strains of the Syndrome. To those who aren't, I can only say that catching average trout from average streams may be a lousy job, but someone has to do it.

CHAPTER TWELVE

Sawhill Portrait

ITS MAIN VIRTUE IS THAT it doesn't demand to be taken seriously. In this way it is unlike the great trout rivers, the southern bass lakes, the Northwest Territories, the Florida Keys, and other places where the devout gather with clenched teeth and steady eyes. That's not to say it can't or shouldn't be taken seriously, of course. Like all waters haunted by fishermen, it conceals great truths. At those times when the whole evening is the color of the shade under a cottonwood at noon, and whatever is about to happen has just begun to unfold, even the little bluegills can seem like the very meaning of your life.

Or not. It's entirely up to you.

There are thirteen ponds, old quarry pits that filled with water, sprouted cattails, attracted waterfowl and shorebirds, and otherwise did what nature intended for holes in the ground to do. Some of the fish were stocked, while others seem merely to have arrived in that uncanny way they have. Someone once said the entire surface of the earth is covered with bullhead eggs which hatch the minute they're covered with water. Fine, but where do carp come from?

An old feller once told me frogs and panfish travel from pond to pond as eggs stuck to the legs of herons. The turtles walk. It sounds plausible, but even old fellers have been known to be mistaken.

For whatever reason, there are largemouth bass, crappies, bluegills galore, pumpkinseeds, rock bass, as well as chubs, carp, and catfish (three creatures that, as a fly-fisher, I find difficult to take seriously).

Still, the trash fish are part of the ambiance of the elaborate warm-water environment, as are dozens of aquatic and terrestrial plants, mammals (from shrews to deer), turtles, frogs, a whole textbook full of insects, and the birds. I've seen ibises there, egrets, avocets aren't uncommon. I don't know my ducks and warblers well enough to say what I've seen in that department. My friend Jack Collom has identified over sixty species of birds there in a single day. Aside from being a crack birder, Jack is a poet — possibly the most famous unknown poet of our time. He's the only nonangler I know who is neither puzzled by, nor overly amused by, the idea that catching fish is the goal but not necessarily the object of angling. "Yes . . . ?" he says, and looks at me questioningly, waiting to hear something that isn't obvious.

Things typically start in April when the bluegills move into the shallows to spawn. Over the past decade or so, the average date has been April 15, coincidentally the deadline for income taxes and therefore easy to remember. Some years it's been a real silver lining.

They can come earlier or later, depending on the shape of a particular season. Over the years I've tried to key the spawning move to such woodsmanlike indicators as the nesting of the Canada geese or the return of the yellow-headed blackbirds, but the fact is, it happens when the water temperature permanently reaches into the mid to high 60s. That's *permanently*. How they can tell the difference between a premature warm spell and the real thing is beyond me, but they can. And I can't.

The plan is to reach that point where I can squint at the sun, sniff the air, listen to the honking of the geese on the first half-warm nights, and know it's time. "Yup, the 'gills ought'a be runnin'." There *is* a certain feel to things when it's on, but so far it's come after the fact. For the time being I'm stuck with scouting.

I go out early in April — late in March if it's been warm — to walk, cast, look, and bobble an aquarium thermometer in the water. The bluegills like shallow coves to spawn in, ones with gravelly bottoms and not much vegetation. In clear water and good light you can see the beds. They're dinner-plate sized and lighter than the surrounding bottom, clustered in groups of from five or six to fifty or more.

The fish use the same areas year after year unless the water is down, so you can go to the old spots, get up on a hill and look, make a few casts, and know in a few minutes. Sometimes when the shallows are empty you can work the deeper water nearby with a sink-tip line and something like a #12 Zug Bug. If the water is, say, 60 degrees, the fish may be congregated out there, waiting.

The best time to start scouting is when it feels too early. When I look at my slides of bluegill fishing, I see pictures of my friends playing fish in steely-looking water; they're wearing wool shirts and denim jackets, the sky is a dark dun color, the trees faint green and sparse, the cattails brown. If you wait for what we think of as spring, you've missed half of it.

Working these ponds at the end of March makes me feel alternately lonely and stupid, wise and cunning — wise to the point of smugness if I come out with a stringer of fish and call A. K., Dave, Bill, Dale, or Paul with *The Word*. Among this small group of bluegilling fly-fishers, it's been left to me to burn up the telephone wires when the fish are up. It's not clear whether this is a tip of the hat to my supposed expertise in the

field or simply that they'd rather be fishing for spawning
rainbows somewhere while I'm looking for the panfish. When
given a choice like that, I tend to consider it a compliment.
These guys get a little less excited about panfish than I do, but
since it's the earliest dependable fishing that can be done with a
flyrod (*dependable*, I said), they perk up when I call.

Along about here I should cop out to the standard outdoor
writer's formula and get into a brief, halfhearted defense of
panfish in general, bluegills in particular. I should say that
they're easy to catch, plentiful, good eating, passable fighters on
light tackle, and custom-made for the fly rod. I should do that,
or rather, I just did.

It's all true. They *are* easy once you find the beds where the
larger fish collect. They guard their nests against each other and
against predators who will happily steal the eggs. These predators
range from dragonfly nymphs to carp. It's a personal theory of
mine that the bedding bluegills, who seem to take no time out
for feeding, survive during the long bedding period on insects
and small fish who try to raid their eggs. Maybe, maybe not. If
true, it would be a typically neat system with lots of carnage and
mutual benefit: the fish survive on the bugs, and the bugs who
don't get eaten (there must be some, or they'd have long since
quit trying) survive for a time on the eggs. It looks like war but
is, in fact, nicely symbiotic. It's like the existence of legalists and
anarchists in the same society. Neither is especially right or
wrong — they're just there, and if there's a larger meaning, it's
to be found in the struggle itself, not in the outcome.

These are the things that can buzz around your head like
mosquitos while you search for the first panfish on a chilly
spring day. Maybe it happens because there are no real
mosquitos to think about.

So much for homespun biological theorizing. It's been
established by people who know that it's almost impossible to
overfish a panfish pond. These little guys overpopulate as a
defense mechanism, and most biologists agree you can't harm a

healthy population with fishing pressure. It might even help, though there seems to be some disagreement about that. What will clearly help is a bunch of big, hungry pike or bass. Carnage and mutual benefit again.

The thirteen ponds hold bass and get some heavy fishing pressure from people who string up their catch. I think the fishing pressure helps the panfish by thinning them but hurts the same population by reducing the number of large predators who eat them. Combine this with cryptic population cycles that can make one year just noticeably better or worse than another and you have a complex chain of interlocking events that results, in this case, in mediocrity. That doesn't detract from the place. Things that are less than perfect have some value in this life, and it's a good thing because there are plenty of them.

The current daily bag limit for bluegills in Colorado is thirty, an embarrassingly impressive stringer even with our modest-sized fish. Out here, a bluegill that covers your hand is unquestionably a keeper. It is a permissible excess, and I guess that's what I like about panfish as much as anything. Later in the season, when the streams come down and the high country opens up, one fishes long and hard for trout. For cultural as well as practical reasons, the trout are seldom kept, which makes a few messes of bluegills in April a pleasant way to start the season — the bounty of spring and all that.

For the record, there is no closed season on fishing in Colorado, a very civilized arrangement. Still, a few frostbite trips to tailwater fisheries for winter trout and the occasional ice-fishing expedition notwithstanding, the "season" begins in April with the panfish.

The thirteen ponds are excellent then, clean and empty. You surprise wildlife and meet only the odd bird watcher or early bait-caster. The latter may greet you with, "What you doin' with that fly rod? There ain't no trout in here."

The place is graspable in a way that a trout stream is not. You can walk around it in an hour or wade or belly boat to every inch of it, with the confidence that you've got them surrounded. At the same time, it's sprawling enough that you can pass a season without having fished it all, partly by choice, partly by oversight.

In early spring you cover ground, surveying the situation. You tie on a weighted wet fly at the truck and never change it, casting it now and then, here and there. It's less a matter of fishing, more a matter of satisfying curiosity. The bluegills are the harbingers, moving early, grouping together to spawn roughly according to size. Often the beds you see, the most exposed ones, are those of the smaller fish. The hand-sized keepers will be nearby, though, in slightly deeper water, safer from herons and kingfishers.

Once you've located the bluegills, you know that the crappies will be established in the deeper, weedier water and that the rock bass will have congregated in various places, especially in the few rocky areas and cement-block riprapped banks — hence their name. Pumpkinseeds, the prettiest fish this side of salt water, seem to spawn alongside the bluegills, though they sometimes develop exclusive areas. Once every spring there's a stringer of all four mixed, a thing so lovely it must be hung from a low tree limb in the late afternoon light and admired as a work of art in which you had a small hand.

Those are the mechanics of early panfishing in Colorado. The same procedures — less casually practiced — work in strange places, too, and one *tries* strange new places because no fisherman is ever satisfied in a lasting way. Still, there's nothing more comfortable than fishing the home water for bluegills and crappies, game fish that go down to the rock bottom of the angler's consciousness as the fish we started on. This business of fishing builds up enormous deposits in the mind, a whole landscape of emotion. On the surface we may see fly rods, dry flies, tweed hats, and such, but if you dig down through it all, past the spinning rods, bait cans, and minnow buckets, you'll find a fossilized bluegill.

There are those fly-fishers who decline to go after panfish (or do go, but exhibit some disdain) because bluegills, crappies, and the rest are seen as kids' fish, lacking the stature of the trouts and bass. Okay, but maybe that's exactly where their charm lies. I mean, how serious do you want to get about this? You try to catch fish as if it really mattered, but you can't lose sight of the fact that it doesn't.

The thirteen ponds are a good place to lose your inflated ideas about yourself as a *fly*-fisher. For one thing, you can take fish on just about any wet fly that isn't too big for the small mouths of panfish. In winters past — the long, cold ones — I've developed a few panfish selections consisting of unnecessarily detailed and realistic warm-water nymphs and free-form fancies, but I'm just as likey now to use up unfished trout flies and unsuccessful experiments in sizes 8, 10, and 12. I once won a five-dollar bet by catching a bluegill on a bare hook (a Mustad 3906-B, size 10, sparsely dressed). This is not what you'd call highly technical match-the-hatching. The fish will hit anything that approaches their territory. Anything. Last spring I spent twenty minutes watching two small pumpkinseeds attacking an 8-pound carp who was vacuuming the eggs from their nest.

You'll also meet a lot of non-fly-fishing types on the ponds, at least later on when the weather has warmed to the first-sunburn-of-the-year stage. Most of these people won't be automatically impressed by you; some will be curious, others amused. If you persist in wearing an up-downer hat over a clean chamois shirt and a bulging, jangling fly vest, you'll begin to feel overdressed. All you need is a Harley Davidson T-shirt, baseball cap, and a small box of wet flies. If you catch fish you may attract some favorable attention, but even then someone will sooner or later kindly inform you that a spinning rod is a hell of a lot easier. Kids will want to take a spin in your belly boat.

So you go on weekdays and stay past suppertime when the crowd flakes away, leaving the "serious" anglers of whatever persuasion to stalk the ponds. Even then, your pretentions dissolve. It slowly dawns on you that your moral stature will not be significantly eroded by easily catching a whole bunch of little fish.

If you start feeling guilty (I seldom do anymore), you can tell yourself it will get plenty hard later. The bass in these very ponds will not come so easy in late May and June. And then there are the trouts. You know about the trouts. They're either taking the *Paraleptophlebia adoptiva* (probably the emerger, possibly the dun) or the smaller *Tricorythodes* spinner. Try the quill-bodies #18 floating nymph — no, not that one, the paler one — on a 12-foot leader with a 7x tippet.

There'll be plenty of that later.

CHAPTER THIRTEEN

Headwaters

AS YOU FOLLOW THE
stream up into the canyon, it seems to get smaller and colder all
at once, an illusion caused by leaving behind the civilized water
where the pools are named and where there are places to park.
Going upstream here, where the cliff forces the road away from
the stream, feels a little like going back in time, and the trout —
still mostly browns — seem as liquid and transparent as the
water. You're elated, still on your first wind.

This is pocket water and there's lots of it — miles and miles
of it — so rather than fish it thoroughly, you keep moving, now
and then casting a dry caddis (an obscure local pattern named
for the stream you're on) over a good-looking spot. It seems
appropriate and it works. Later there will be a hatch of caddis or
maybe even may flies and you'll stop and get down to business,
but since you're more interested in distance now, you fish
casually from the bank in hiking boots with the pack on your
back.

You go carefully because you're walking with the rod strung, sometimes having to thread it through the brush and low limbs ahead. The cloth bag is stuffed in your pants pocket but, in the interest of lightness and mobility, you've left the aluminum case at home.

It's your favorite cane rod, a 7½-footer for a #5 line. You debated over the choice, weighing the risk to the rod against how perfectly suited it was to this little stream. Finally the honey-colored rod with its English reel won out. It's idiotic, you thought, to spend hundreds of dollars on a fine rig that you're afraid to use. And now you're pleased: the wood rod casts beautifully, and through it you can almost feel the heartbeats of the small trout. When you stop for lunch you lean it very carefully against the springy branches of a short blue spruce.

You've been walking easily and haven't gone far, but already it feels good to have the pack off. It's not as light as it could be — they never are — but considering how long you'll be out, it's not bad. You're figuring three days, maybe four, and you were very careful not to say exactly when you'd be back.

You haven't had to rummage in the pack yet, so it still seems a model of efficiency, ever so slightly virginal, leaning in the shade of a lichen-covered ledge. Tied on top are the rolled-up sleeping pad and the poncho which can be worn to cover you and all the gear or made into a serviceable free-form rain fly. The down sleeping bag is tied to the bottom and the old number 44 "Cold Handle" frying pan is strapped securely to the back. The pan always seems a little too big, but it will hold two butterfly-filleted, 8- to 12-inch trout perfectly. You'll eat fish on this trip or come back early; your provisions are composed of just-add-water starches and soups with some coffee, one can of pork and beans (a treat), some oil, salt, pepper, and lemon juice. Side dishes. The main courses are still in the water.

Beyond that, there isn't much: clothing you can wear all at once if necessary (wool shirt, sweater, down vest, wool hat), coffeepot, fork and spoon, spare socks, flyweight waders, wading shoes (low-cut tennis shoes, actually, because they're smaller and lighter than the real thing), and your tin cup. It's in the side pocket now, but if you were farther north you'd tie it next to the frying pan as a bear bell. Packed in the coffee cup is a heavy plastic bag to put the tennis shoes in once they're wet.

There's a camera in there, too, and the pack is so pretty in the mottled shade you think about digging it out and taking a shot, but it's only a thought. At the moment you don't feel like looking at the world through a piece of glass, even an expensive piece.

The only luxuries you've allowed yourself are a full-sized coffeepot, a notebook, and a modest-sized bottle of good bourbon — but maybe they're not entirely luxuries, at that. The coffeepot doubles as a saucepan, and holds enough water to completely douse the campfire in three trips to the stream. Your life has been such that there's the normal background noise of guilt, but so far, you haven't burned down a forest and don't plan to; you are meticulously careful with your fires.

The bourbon is still in the glass bottle because it just doesn't taste right from the lighter plastic flask, and whether the whiskey itself is a luxury or a necessity isn't worth worrying about at the moment. The notebook might be considered nonessential except that you generally use more of its pages to start fires than to jot down lines of poetry and notes of cosmic significance.

After lunch — a deli ham-and-cheese sandwich in waxed paper — you put the rod in the bag and walk. The trail is gone now, and the country is more rugged. Dippers splash in the stream; you spook a doe mule deer coming around a bend; and you get very close to a marmot sunning on a rock before he wakes up and bolts, giving the warning whistle, even though he seems to be alone.

At one point you find yourself within five feet of a pair of typically innocent blue grouse. You consider the possibility of getting one with a rock and have a momentary olfactory hallucination: roasting grouse and frying trout. You decide against it, though, probably because it's illegal.

And then it's late afternoon, the canyon has begun to level out a little, and the stream has a distinct shady side. The pocket water has given way to a long run, the bank on one side of which is open and grassy. There are delicious-looking undercuts. With several hours of daylight left, you find a level spot away from the stream (away from mosquitos and morning dew or frost) and lean the pack against a tree, unroll the sleeping bag to air out, clean out a fire pit, gather wood, and set out coffeepot, frying pan, and tin cup.

The spot you've chosen is a tiny meadow stretch only a few hundred yards long. The open sky is pleasant after the closed-in, forested canyon below, and ahead, for the first time today, you can see the snowcapped high country. The weather is still shirt-sleeve warm with a comfortable hint of evening chill. There is as much spruce and fir as pine now on the hillsides, and you can see patches of aspen. You think you hear the screech of a hawk but see nothing when you scan the sky.

You could probably fish the stream here without wading, but you dig out the waders and put them on because you carried them in and are gonna use them; it's important. There's no fly vest; instead, you're wearing a four-pocketed canvas fishing shirt which you load now from the side pocket of the pack: three spools of leader material in the lower right-hand pocket, bug dope, fly floatant, and clippers in the lower left. Each breast pocket holds a fly box — one with nymphs and streamers, the other with dries. In the interest of razor-sharp efficiency, you wanted to have a single box, but the bigger ones didn't fit anywhere and you only toyed for a few minutes with the idea of rebuilding the fishing shirt. Anyhow, the bulges are more symmetrical this way.

You saw two small rises at the tail of the run when you first arrived, and now you notice what looks like a bigger fish working along the far grassy bank. There are a few tan-colored bugs that you assume are caddis flies fluttering over the surface,

but without pondering the situation further, you tie on a #16
Tan-Bodied Adams. The trout in these mountain streams see few
anglers and are seldom selective (though your two fly boxes are
evidence of the occasional exceptions) and the Tan Adams is a
favorite. The tails are of medium-dark moose body hair, the
body of light raccoon fur; the grizzly hackle is mixed with ginger
instead of brown, and the wings are wide and darkly barred —
from a hen neck. It's a personal variation you often think of as a
"generic bug," an excellent high-country pattern.

You work the tail of the run first and, on the third cast, take a
tiny rainbow that still has his parr marks, a wild fish. Then you
take a slightly larger one that wasn't rising but came up to your
fly anyway, and then you take the fish along the bank — a 9-
inch brown.

The fish are eager, slightly stupid, and not large; you get a
strike nearly every time you put a good cast over a rising trout.
Then you land and release a fine, chubby, 10-inch brown and
remember what a friend once said: "If you're gonna keep fish, go
ahead and keep 'em. If you wait till the last two, you'll be eating
beans." So the next good fish, a fat, bright rainbow of 10 or 11
inches, is tapped on the head and tossed on the bank in the
direction of camp. This is something you seldom do anymore,
but it doesn't feel too bad. In fact, it feels pretty good.

After five or six more fish, you take a firm brown that reaches
the full 12 inches from the butt of the reel seat to the first T in
the name on the rod. It's a male with a slightly hooked jaw and
colors that remind you of a Midwestern autumn. You clean him,
along with the rainbow, wrap them both in wet grass, and lay
them in the shadows that have now swallowed the stream and
half the eastern ridge. You're camped on the west bank to catch
the first morning sunlight.

You think of going to a streamer then, of running it past the
undercut to see if there's a big brown there, but the dry fly and
the wood rod are too hypnotic. You take a few more small fish
and quit with just enough light left to get situated in camp. You

clip the tattered and now one-winged fly from the leader and drop it in the stream, like you'd smash a glass after a toast.

Supper is trout fried in oil with pepper and lemon juice, rice, and whiskey cut lightly with stream water — eaten by firelight. Then, lying in the down bag, you let the fire die to coals, think of the trout, the hike, home, people, career, the past, and you are asleep.

The morning is gray and cold, but blue holes perforate the clouds to the west. You put on the wool shirt and vest, build a fire, and start water for coffee. After one cup you go to the stream, waderless, and without ceremony take one 9-inch rainbow for breakfast. You roast him over the fire on a stick so as not to dirty the pan, and on another stick you make Bisquick muffins — a bit dry, but just fine. As someone (probably French) once said, "Hunger is the best sauce."

With the fire well doused and the pack loaded, you take one careful look around to make sure nothing was dropped or forgotten, then head off upstream with only a single look back at that undercut bank where you never did try a streamer.

By midmorning the sun is out, and you stop to shed some clothes before you get too sweaty. While putting the stuff in the pack, you're struck with the sudden certainty that you forgot the roll of nylon cord with which you can turn your poncho into whatever-shaped rain fly the terrain and handy trees allow; you can clearly picture it lying on the kitchen table at home. But then a short, carefully unfrantic search turns up the cord, as well as an apple you'd forgotten about. At least one attack of backpacker's paranoia per trip is normal, but you don't mind because it has served you well. You've never forgotten anything important.

With the rhythm of the walk broken, you decide to fish, and with the Tan Adams you take the first brook trout. But since you've taken only two other small fish after fifteen minutes, you shoulder the pack and move on.

Shortly you come to a road and, although it breaks the spell a little, you're glad it's there. On the way out you'll climb the grade and hitch a ride to the nearest cafe for pancakes or maybe a big, greasy burger, and then on into town. But now you go under the bridge with the stream, listening for the whine of a car and being glad not to hear one.

Above the road you come into a high, marshy meadow. Here the trees stop as the land levels out, giving way to tangles of willow; the only way to walk through it is up the stream, in waders. Wading and casting with the pack on and the hiking shoes dangling in back is clumsy but not impossible. You work only the best-looking spots at first, slowing down and concentrating a little more after you've spooked some good fish from what looked like uninteresting water. The trout are brookies now, with the occasional rainbow.

By the time you hit the beaver ponds, your back aches from the pack; so you set up camp on the first level, dry spot you come to. After a short break, you switch to a streamer and creep down to the nearest pond. The fly is a little brook trout bucktail, and your past success with it has convinced you that brookies do, in fact, eat their smaller relatives, even though more than one fisheries biologist has told you that's not so. You think, science. *Truth*. The fish take the fly, so it's true; or maybe it's largely false but still works, and so might as well be true — like politics or religion. It occurs to you that the Great Questions are probably a hell of a lot more fun than the answers, but by the time you've made your fifth cast, you've forgotten about the whole thing.

Four ponds and a dozen fair-to-middling trout later, you hook a heavy fish back in some flooded brush — a *heavy* fish. He fights well but stays in the open, where you play him carefully. You wish you'd brought a net, even though you'd have snagged it in the brush two-hundred times by now. You play the fish out more than you'd like to, finally hand landing him as gently as possible. As you hold him by the lower jaw to remove the barbless hook, he wiggles and his teeth cut into your thumb, starting a small stain of blood in the water.

Laid against the rod, the trout's tail reaches well past the 12-inch mark, well past. Sixteen inches? Possibly, and fat, too, and deeply, richly colored; the orange flanks are like a neon beer sign shining through a rainy night. You sit there like an idiot until the trout's struggles indicate that he's recovered from the fight. You release him then, and he swims away, leaving you with a momentary sense of absolute blankness, as if the synapses in your brain marked "good" and "bad" had fired simultaneously, shorting each other out.

Then you're hungry, and cold. You backtrack down the channel below the pond and keep the first three small trout you hook, trying to picture the exact size of the frying pan. Supper is eaten in chilly twilight; the waders are hung to dry; the rod, in its cloth case, is hung out of reach of porcupines who would chew up the cork grip for the salt, given half a chance. The dishes are washed, by feel, in muddy gravel.

The next morning you wake before dawn, soaking wet, freezing, and covered with mosquito bites, having slept dreamlessly on the edge of a bog through a substantial rain, with the poncho lying uselessly under you as a ground cloth. The curses you utter — the foulest ones you can think of — are the first words you've spoken aloud in two days.

Luckily the sky is clear now, and the sun comes up warm over the eastern ridge, helping along the effects of the smoky fire that took fifteen minutes to start. You recover by degrees, aided by coffee, and drape your gear in the willows to dry, everything angled to face the sun like the heads of flowers. Even the notebook was damp, towards the back, so you started the fire with pages that were written on, pages you did not read before lighting.

Breakfast is big and starchy, mostly half-ruined rice mixed with pond-water chicken soup, a shapeless candy bar you found while emptying the pack, and the apple. The candy bar wrapper is burned in the fire, but the apple core is tossed in the brush

for a squirrel or maybe an elk. After fluffing and turning the
sleeping bag, you slog the half mile to the head of the ponds and
fish the stream, where you hook the first cutthroat — small,
bright, and confused looking. You feel a little more in touch
with the place, having been soaked and frozen with, apparently,
no ill effects.

Back in gear — the pack tight, dry, and efficient again — you
leave the stream and hike the dry ridge side towards the lake.
Most of the time you can't even see the stream in its tunnels of
tangled willow. You're moving well, feeling free on the dry
ground in the shady spruce and fir, sensing the curves and cups
of the land now instead of the bottom of the trough where the
water runs.

You angle up unconsciously (almost always better to gain
altitude than lose it when walking in the mountains) and come
on the lake a little high, from a vantage point of no more than
fifty extra feet. You wouldn't have planned that just for the
view, but the view is excellent, with the small lake hanging in its
tight cirque, smooth and blue-gray, with snowfields on the
western slope and a soft-looking lawn of tundra around it. The
trees here are short and flagged, bare of branches on the
windward side.

You set up camp on a perfect, level spot, rigging a clumsy rain
fly (thinking of last night) though the sky is cloudless. It seems
early, *is* early, in fact, but the looming Continental Divide means
dusk will come before it seems right. You stroll down to the
outlet, the logical place for fish to be since the inlet is only
snowmelt from a scree slope, and sure enough, you spot a few
rising cutts. You've tied on a #16 Michigan Chocolate Spinner,
based on previous experience, time of day, location, and hunch.
You've also put on the wool shirt and hat because it's cool away
from the shelter of the trees.

You stalk up to the water too quickly, too erect, and the trout
don't exactly spook but solemnly stop rising. They don't know
what you are, but they don't like you — a thought that cuts

through the magazine-feature-article glitter of wildeness fly-
fishing for the ten minutes it takes for two of the smaller fish to
start feeding again.

The first cast is a good one, straight and sure with a
downstream hook on the admittedly easy, uniform current, and
a 13-inch cutt takes the spinner with a casual, unsuspicious rise.
The fight is good, but because the fish has no place to go, you
land him easily. It's supper and the last fish of the day; the
others have vanished in that supernatural way trout have — they
don't run like deer or fly away like grouse; they're just gone.

In camp you fry the trout, sitting close to the fire that seems
to give little heat in the thin air. Camping alone isn't something
you normally do, but you've done it often enough that it's
familiar; you no longer get the horrors at night. You've gone out
alone before because you were sad or happy, or neither or both
— for any reason at all, the way some people drink. The lake is
black now, and for a long moment you can't remember why
you're here this time.

CHAPTER FOURTEEN

Turning Pro

THE WAITRESS DOWN at the cafe gave me a short lecture about having nothing but a donut and four cups of coffee for breakfast — "That's not a very nutritious way to start your day, you know" — and I responded with less-than-perfect courtesy. Sorry about that, Agnes. I was slightly hung over from celebrating something or other the night before and a little edgy about the number of flies I had to have tied by the end of the week. The bright spot that morning was the state of the world as reported in the *Rocky Mountain News*: maybe they'd drop the Big One soon and put me out of my misery.

Back at home I turned on the radio. I usually listen to rock and roll while tying flies (there's something about all that raw sexual energy that makes me work faster), but on the morning in question I decided on some quieter classical music. This big batch of dry flies was not going to go quickly, but then a journey of a thousand miles begins with a single step, right?

By the time I located the bobbin with the 6/0 olive thread where the cat had hidden it under the couch, the chamber music had stopped and a woman with a grating, nasal voice was talking about prenatal care in the Third World countries. I left it on, knowing that if I stopped to hunt up a better station I'd decide to brew a pot of coffee, notice that the dishes needed washing, and be launched on a course of procrastination that could well end up eight hours later and thirty miles away.

The first fly was a genuine clunker, one for the Mason jar I keep on a shelf over the tying desk. When the jar gets about a quarter of an inch deep, I donate the flies, anonymously, to the local fishing club raffle. The second fly was acceptable, and the third was actually kind of pretty in spite of everything. Half an hour later I was tying at something like cruising speed and learning more than I cared to know about what it's like to be pregnant in Africa — no fun, apparently.

No, I don't *hate* tying flies; it's just that, as with any job, some days go better than others. Tying for money, however you approach it, is a business venture complete with the appropriate problems: checks that bounce or don't come at all, periods of feast and famine, deadlines, capital expenditures, raspy customers, and days when you should have stayed in bed. Any time you turn a hobby into a profession, you step from one reality into another.

My initiation into commercial tying was much like that of other tiers I know. I had made my own flies for a number of years and was, in all modesty, competent. When I turned out a dozen #14 Adamses, they all looked pretty much alike and were comparable to the ones you'd buy in a fly shop. Never mind how long it took me to tie them.

I had learned to tie at my own slow, plodding pace with occasional great leaps forward — revelations, really — provided by good books or, better yet, the helpful advice and counsel of good tiers. I had assembled all the basic tools (along with a drawerful of doodads that were supposed to have revolutionized fly-tying but didn't), as well as what I thought was a fairly extensive inventory of hooks and materials. I was, in other words, a serious and established amateur flytier.

My first order came from a friend who wanted a few dozen dry midge patterns (22s and 24s) that the one fly shop in the area back then didn't carry. I took it on because I was flattered. I didn't charge him enough and, as I recall, even threw in a cheap little plastic fly box — innocent, puppyish gestures. As Agnes down at the cafe says, "Flattery will get you anything."

Many of the tiers I know had the same experience with that first order. They felt that they'd relinquished their amateur status but, as with other cases of lost innocence, it was less than a big deal when it finally happened: trumpets didn't sound and the earth didn't move; they just sold a few dozen flies and spent the money at the liquor store or the gas station, whichever they passed first.

Still, although it wasn't what you could call the dawn of a new day, that first order did raise a whole field of possibilities. A guy could make a few bucks at this, buy a new cane rod that he doesn't really need, maybe a belly boat. On the other hand, it had taken me quite a while to tie those few dozen flies. When I worked it out it came to about half the current minimum wage.

Clearly, speed was the answer, and the next few small orders taught me that speed doesn't come from hurrying; it comes from counting out your hooks, sizing all your hackles, pairing wings, and otherwise laying out your materials beforehand, then tying one "perfect" fly at a time — relaxed, methodical concentration.

You'll naturally get faster with practice but will just as naturally level out at some point. I've never been able to better my top speed of something like a dozen and a half per hour, not counting preparation time, for standard winged, hackled dries. Simple unweighted nymphs might run closer to two dozen an hour. That seems to be about rock bottom for turning a decent profit, but if I try to push it past that, I screw up and my hourly production actually drops.

Then, somewhere along the line, I came to the awful
realization that I'd run out of materials and that whatever money
had come in in small increments had gone wherever it is pocket
change goes.

Well, I wasn't exactly *out* of materials; I still had boxes of
stuff, but the sizes 12 through 20 hackles (in dun, brown, ginger,
and grizzly), standard hooks in the same sizes, hen necks and
mallard flank for wings, neck butts for striped quill bodies, and
the like were picked clean. I was okay on weird-colored flosses
and fluorescent bucktails, but nobody in Northern Colorado
wanted steelhead patterns; they wanted Elk Hair Caddises, Red
Quills, Blue Duns.

I replaced that stuff over the counter at the fly shop, and it
cost me a fair piece of change. I've since learned that even if you
don't buy enough at a crack to warrant wholesale prices, you can
sometimes get in on the edge of bulk orders or get together with
a group of local part-timers and put in your own.

At that point I'd probably broken even or maybe even gone
into the black a little, though there was no way to tell for sure
because I hadn't kept track of it. The only thing I was certain of
was that I'd become a better, faster tier.

You learn a lot about tying flies by tying a lot of them. I don't
think I've ever really nailed a pattern that I haven't tied ten or
twenty dozen of, and the things you learn are close to
indescribable: that certain tension on the thread, for instance, as
you tighten on a pair of wings and even the angle of those wings
on the hook shank that allows for the torque of the thread,
cocking them right on top every time; how to pinch off just
enough dubbing for a #16 body; the precise angle at which the
hackle feathers are tied in.

On an Elk Hair Caddis, a pattern I'm tying at the moment, I
find that once I'm cooking, I can pinch just the right amount of
elk hair from the skin so that when I brush out the underfur and
the few hairs that inevitably come with it, I end up with just the
right-sized clump for the wing. Once it's stacked I measure it for

length against the hook shank and then, I just recently noticed, I roll it back almost imperceptibly in my fingers so that when I trim it I've added a tiny fraction of an inch. It still comes out right. In fact, it wouldn't come out right otherwise. I don't know how long I've been doing that, but it works, and it has the unmistakable feel of the subconscious about it. Now I'm trying hard not to think about it for fear of losing the touch.

Of course the only way to find out if you're ready to tie at a truly professional level is to give it a shot and see what happens. I took my shot one winter when I took on, in addition to everything else, an order for 160 dozen dry flies. I figured it was time to quit fooling around and actually make some money. The flies were all variants, simply quill-bodied flies that don't even have wings, something that seemed to balance out the numbers somehow.

Prior to this, drudgery had never been a big problem for me. Oh, I'd gotten behind a few times and had had to rush to catch up, but I could always see the end of it: that last dozen flies, the cold beer as a reward (I learned early that I shouldn't drink beer while tying), and finally the check. That's the beauty of small orders.

Big orders, on the other hand, are more like trying to empty a bathtub with a spoon and are, at times at least, about as interesting. I finished that one with more relief than satisfaction. You know how a word or phrase becomes meaningless when it's repeated often enough? The same thing happens when you tie 1,920 flies of the same pattern — variant, variant, variant, variant, variant, variant, variant, variant, variant, variant . . .

My other work hadn't suffered much more than it usually does from periodic attacks of sloth or cabin fever, but I couldn't shake the feeling that if I'd put in that much time at the typewriter over the winter, I might have produced the next great regional American novel (which might have been picked up by Hollywood, and by now I could be smoking big cigars and walking the streets with a starlet on each arm). But then, that's just my particular hangup.

That was also the year I never quite got my own fly boxes filled and had to tie countless frantic half dozens of this and that over the summer. That's not an uncommon problem for professional tiers, though I'll have to admit that my fly selection program falls somewhere between paranoia and naked greed. I've never had all the flies I wanted, probably never will, and couldn't carry them if I did.

I also began to see that if I were going to turn pro in a serious way, I'd have to gear up. A full-time professional tier should have on hand a full range of hooks and materials *in bulk*, both for the price break you get buying that way and because you can't afford to go out and hunt up the materials for every order that comes along. It's the kind of thing you can ease into, but even easing involves what, to an amateur tier, looks like some serious money.

Then, of course, a large volume of materials presents storage and organization problems requiring shelves and cases of moth balls, and looming on the horizon are things like stationery, business cards, shipping boxes, long-distance phone bills, a bookkeeping system, tax records, etc.

Front money? Bookkeeping? Taxes!? How about tying flies all summer when you should be fishing? Maybe this is getting out of hand. A successful professional tier is a craftsman to be sure, but he's also a competent businessman, and that's the part that finally stopped me. Running a small business suits some people, but I am among those it does *not* suit.

I guess what I really wanted out of professional tying, aside from a little money, was professional *status*, that hip, mildly amused, worldly, pipe-puffing, your-name-on-a-coffee-cup-down-at-the-fly-shop mystique. What I didn't want was endless hours slaving over a hot vise. It reminds me of the flirtation I once had with being a rock-and-roll guitar player — I liked the money, girls, and free drinks but didn't want to pay my dues by practicing four hours a day.

In the end it became obvious that it was a matter of temperament. You can make a decent living at fly tying if it suits you, but I can work harder, longer, and with better results at other things, so that's what I do. One of the reasons I'm in here typing right now instead of in the other room tying those Elk Hair Caddises is that a writer can be sipping a beer and looking out the window and still be "working." Temperament.

I haven't given it up, mind you; I've just drifted out to the edge of the local fly-tying scene where I take on some modest orders for the shops and hold on to a handful of regular customers. The money is negligible, I suppose, but it does pay for the materials for my own flies (which I now have time to tie) with enough left over that I'm thinking of buying a canoe this year.

It's comfortable, mostly, which is as it should be with something you enjoy but don't care to make a life's work of. Now and then, as I'm storing the clothes for one season and digging out those for another, I come across my guitar up in the attic and recall the time I said, for the four-hundredth time, "If you have any requests, keep 'em to yourselves, 'cause we prob'ly don't know 'em, yuk, yuk, yuk," and realized that I'd put something I loved right down the toilet without even getting rich in the process.

Everyone should do that once in his life to learn the lesson, but once is enough.

CHAPTER FIFTEEN

The Fly Rod

IT WAS A HOT
afternoon in July when I stopped in at the tackle shop to bum a
cup of coffee and kill a little time before hitting the river. The
air was dry and still, the clouds sparse, high, and unmoving —
the kind of day when the big tan caddis flies would come off
well in that hour or so that begins with kingfishers and ends
with bats.

Harry, the owner of the place, materialized out of the clutter
and came over to greet me warmly — not the usual procedure.
He had a conniving grin on his face that I recognized
immediately. "Hey, it's a good thing you came in," he said, "I've
got some rods I know you'll be interested in and they're gonna
go fast."

Now Harry is the kind of carnivore you'll run into in the
tackle business from time to time. To him customers are a prey
species and he'd try to sell an anchor to a drowning man
because he just got them in and they're gonna go fast.

I wasn't really in the mood to fend off the high-pressure sales pitch I could see coming, but then I *had* come in to kill time and I'll always look at rods. Harry led me into the back room where I poured a cup of evil-smelling coffee while he produced, with exaggerated care, a dozen aluminum cases. "An*tique* cane fly rods," he said with a leer. "Some old guy died and his son gave me the whole batch on consignment. I'm lettin' em go real cheap."

It was quite a collection. All the rods were top production models by well-known makers, all obviously used but just as obviously well cared for. Of the dozen, most were trout rods, and these showed the most wear, but there were also two heavy sticks you'd have to call salmon rods and a couple more that were probably intended for bass. They weren't an*tiques*, but they were lovely.

I went through the trout rods one by one, putting them together and wiggling them tentatively. I became so engrossed that Harry's droning pitch began to sound like an overhead conversation in a foreign language — a conversation laced with English terms like "collector's item" and "investment."

It was inevitable that one rod would catch my eye, and when Harry saw that happen he invented some chore out front in order to let me stew in private. There was no choice, really. The rod was clearly the hardest used of the batch and, although Harry probably figured I'd spotted it as the bargain, it was actually something else. This had clearly been the favorite rod of someone who had had a lot of fine ones to choose from and I just wanted to wiggle it some more, maybe to try to feel a little of the magic.

It was a 7-foot, two-piece made of light cane the color of dry weeds in late winter, the wraps were bright red, and the cap and ring reel seat was nickel silver and — oak? — too dark, butternut maybe. You could see where the ring had been snugged up against the foot of the same reel countless times. The grip and seat were in miniature; my hand covered the cork and slopped over a little.

It was a light, floppy rod, about a 3 weight, I guessed, made back when those delicate noodles were all the rage with the tweed-and-cane types. I wondered how it could have been the favorite of someone with so many equally fine and much more reasonable 5 and 6 weights.

So the guy had been a crank, but a crank with good taste. I might have liked him, and I was clearly coming to like that ridiculous little rod. I tried to be amused by it but — I don't know — I just had this *feeling*.

I found myself wondering why the son would just up and dispose of something that had obviously meant so much to his father. To me they were fine old rods, but to him they should have been heirlooms, a legacy. Well, maybe the kid was just an ungrateful shit or seriously strapped for cash. Those things happen, and it wasn't my problem. My problem, suddenly, was to get Harry to part with the thing for less than an arm and a leg, even though I had no idea of what I'd do with it.

So, I bought it.

Over the next few days I showed it around to some friends (most of whom were duly impressed) and then leaned it in the corner with the rest of my rods, where it stayed for about two weeks before it started making me nervous.

It was a nagging, uneasy feeling like when you know you're forgetting something important but can't figure out what it is. It had to do with the rod somehow, and I thought maybe it was that I'd bought it without really intending to fish it. I had a .22 rifle that I seldom shot anymore and a few rods that didn't get fished much, but I wasn't what you'd call a collector. I'd always intended to use the gear I bought, it's just that sometimes it didn't work out that way. You know how it is.

As time went by it bugged me more and more. Sometimes at night when I was tying flies that rod case leaning in the corner behind me would give me a creepy feeling. A few days of that and I was back at Harry's looking for a 3-weight line.

When I told Harry what I wanted, the son-of-a-bitch grinned like a hungry vampire, vanished into the back room, and emerged, after rummaging around noisily for ten minutes, with an old but well-kept English reel loaded with a number three, double-taper braided silk line. He said it had been in a box of odd stuff that had come with the rods and was, without doubt, the very line that went with the one I'd bought.

Normally I'd have told Harry to shove his silk line but — and I can't really explain this — somehow it seemed appropriate; in fact, it seemed perfect, though I'd never fished a silk line in my life.

At any other time I'd have insisted on buying just the line (I had spare spools at home), but when Harry refused to "break up the set," my sales resistance just melted, to his delight. I spent the whole drive home wondering what the hell I'd just done.

The rod was slower and lighter than anything I was used to, and even after casting it for half an hour along the fence out back, I couldn't quite get the hang of it. I was trying to be kind, too. Still, I figured I'd better fish it at least once, having suckered myself into buying the line.

The band notched comfortably against the worn spot on the foot of the reel — so it *was* the one.

To keep a long story short, I couldn't make the rod work. I spent a half hour at the Bridge Pool slapping the water, throwing tailing loops into wind knots, hooking my hat, and piling casts at my feet like an amateur. Up in the riffle at the head of the pool, I managed to get two strikes from little trout and learned that the rod had no backbone for setting hooks.

That evening I wiped it off and put it away with a feeling of finality. It was still a nice old piece to have, I told myself, and maybe in a few years I could turn a profit on it.

That was that for a couple of weeks, but then the rod started making me nervous again. I can't explain it, but when I was tying flies I could sense it back there in the corner behind me, and when I'd take one of my other rods from the stack of cases, it

would seem to be glaring at me from the back of the pile where
it had migrated from disuse. It was the only rod case I had with
that brass cap, and it stuck out like a sore thumb.

A couple of weeks after I'd fished the rod and decided I
didn't like it, a couple of the boys came out to fish the Blue-
Quill hatch. Without thinking about it, I grabbed the rod and
said, "I think I'll fish the old 3-weight today." The strange thing
was that I didn't want to fish the rod at all; I'd had the 8-foot-5
weight in mind. It was like I'd lost control of what I was doing,
like when you have too many at a party and make a pass at a
friend's wife in spite of yourself.

I struggled with the rod all day, keeping to myself to avoid
embarrassment, and as we were having a few beers on the front
porch that evening, I learned that I was the only one in our party
who'd gotten skunked. So I lied, allowing as how I'd had an off
day but had managed to land three browns. It was one of those
glorious early fall evenings with a clear, cloudless sunset and a
pleasant chill in the air. My friends bought the lie without
question, and I felt like hell.

Not long after that, dove season opened. After doves came
grouse, then pheasants, ducks, and geese, and then rabbits
around the turn of the year. The rod didn't bother me again
until I tried to sell it.

It was in February, always a tough month, when I got low on
cash. I had money coming in from some orders of flies, but it
was late and I needed more hooks and feathers, not to mention
some groceries. I called up the newspaper and took out an ad
offering the rod for sale, but when it came out, they'd printed
my phone number wrong. I complained, and the woman said
they'd make the correction and run it again the following week
for free. "No problem," I said.

When the ad came out the next week, the number was right
but the phone was out of order. Seems a cottonwood had fallen
on the line up in the canyon somewhere, and it was hard to get
to. The repairman said it was funny, as the tree wasn't old or

rotten, it hadn't been struck by lightning, and there'd been no wind. Not one of the great mysteries of the universe, but odd.

The phone stayed dead until the ad ran out, and by then I'd sold a camera, had gotten a check for some flies, and had traded a few dozen bucktails for some venison. Okay, never mind.

By spring I'd forgotten about the whole thing. Well, I hadn't forgotten, exactly, but had pretty much written it off to stress caused by the unconscious fear of nuclear disaster or some such thing. I resolved to eat a little better, drink a little less, and stop reading newspapers.

As the weather began to break, I tied flies like they were going out of style and got in some fishing for bass and bluegills, but then, when the river came down and the trout fishing started, I began to get that nervous feeling again. The first time it really hit me — that damned rod case sulking back there in the corner — I stuck it in a closet full of winter coats and snowshoes and felt better.

Then, a few days later, I had a dream. I'd been up late tying hoppers, and when I finally got to bed I drifted in and out of sleep, still tying flies in my head and seeing bunches of elk hair every time I rolled over. When I did drop off, in the not-so-small hours of the morning, I dreamed there was an old, white-haired man wandering around the house. He was dressed in chest waders and a floppy cloth hat, and he seemed to be looking for something. He walked with a limp — not a bad-leg limp, more of a sore-foot limp — and after he'd gone through the kitchen and the front room, he shuffled down the hall, opened the closet, and took the rod case out. He pushed his hat back on his head, pulled the rod out, and stood there looking at it for a long time, turning it over and over in his hands.

The next morning I woke up late but still felt like I hadn't had enough sleep. I made a point of starting the coffee before I went in and checked the closet. The rod was still there. Of course it's still there, I thought, where the hell did you think it would be?

I put it out of my mind, with some effort, but the next night I had the same dream. In the morning I told myself firmly that I was not spooked and resolved not to give in and check the closet again. I knew the rod was there. Hell, I could *feel* it in there. But then, as I walked down the hall, I noticed that the closet door was open a few inches. I told myself I just hadn't closed it all the way the day before, though that's not how I remembered it.

I went over to Harry's that afternoon intending to ask him if he'd had anything funny happen with the rods, but I realized it wasn't a good idea as soon as I walked in the door. After all, what did I mean by "funny"?

As he followed me around the shop like an Arab beggar trying to sell me all kinds of useless junk (the easy sale on the reel and line had been like the scent of blood to him), I did manage to ease the conversation, such as it was, around to the rods. Harry told me the guy who'd brought them in, the son of the old man who'd died, had come in a week ago, announced that he was leaving town, and had sold the remaining rods for a song. "He really seemed to want to get rid of them," Harry said, beaming.

"Do you know his name?" I asked.

"Don't remember. Baker, Barker, somethin' like that."

"Where did he live?"

"Don't know. Hey, listen, I'm closin' out these belly boats . . ."

I extracted myself from Harry's and drove over to the cafe out where the road crosses the river and ordered a special. While I was poking at a plate of greenish-brown meatloaf, I happened to glance at the old painting they have on the wall down there.

It's a bad painting of a fly-fisherman that I must have seen a thousand times but never really looked at twice. The mountains look flat, the water looks more like snow, and the fisherman (who's all out of proportion) is holding a mayfly the size of a sparrow on his finger. It's the kind of thing that passes for art only if the painter lives next door.

I don't know how long I stared at it before it registered that the fisherman was the old man in the dream — floppy hat, waders, and all. The meatloaf started to crawl around on the plate like a snail.

When Sarah came over to refill my coffee, even though I hadn't touched it, I asked about the painting. Turned out her father had done it, and she thought it was beautiful.

"Who's the fisherman?" I asked.

"That's right," she said, "you wouldn't remember Old Dell."

The story of Old Dell Barker, with one interruption when a truck driver came in, went something like this:

He'd lived over in town with his wife and son years ago, but everyone up here knew him then because he was a hot fisherman and was on the river every weekend between the end of runoff and dove season. No one knew what he did for a living, but apparently it was pretty good because he always dressed well, drove an expensive car, and fished with good tackle. Tipped well in the cafe, too.

Then, one summer, he started showing up during the week as well, and folks noticed that his clothes had gotten a little ratty and he'd quit washing his car. In August of that year, must have been '55 or '56, Sarah figured, he moved into that little cabin just downstream from me. It's a ruin now, burned. Sarah said she thought some kids smoking pot had set it on fire.

Dell kept to himself so folks had to piece together what happened. Apparently he just moved out one day, taking nothing but his fly rods, shotguns, and a few other odds and ends; when his wife finally got around to divorcing him a year or so later, he gave her everything (and there was plenty, I guess) without batting an eye. People figured he'd just flipped out, though no one really knew.

Sarah's early memories of him were of a slightly stooped but mostly healthy-looking white-haired man who lived alone, fished constantly in season and, some said, drank a bit. The kids were scared of him, but most people kind of liked him, or at least thought of him as harmless.

The trucker left, and Sarah got a cup of coffee and sat down in the booth across from me.

"I guess Dell was rich once," she said, "but all the time he lived here he was poor as a church mouse, although they say he had a bunch of fancy fly rods up in that cabin that was worth thousands of dollars."

"So what ever happened to him?" I asked.

"Stroke. He went into the county nursing home about eight years ago, laid there like a sack of shit until early this year, and then died. I saw the thing in the paper, the obituary."

Sarah was quiet for a few minutes. Then she looked out the window at the river and got a kind of shy smile on her face.

"He was an ornery old bastard," she said. "He and my dad were sort of friends; I mean, they weren't *buddies* or anything, but they fished together sometimes. Anyway, one time Dell ordered this little-bitty fly rod from back East somewhere — no telling where he got the money — and Dad told him only a sissy would fish with a little thing like that. Well, Dell's feelings were hurt; he got real insulted. He started fishing that little rod all the time, just to show Dad, and damned if he didn't fish with nothing but that one little rod for just about the rest of his life, I mean, until he fell over that day over by the Island Pool. He fished one of those old-style silk lines, too, and Dad gave him a lot of crap about that. Dad was the only one I ever saw talk to Old Dell more than just to say hello. So what's wrong with the meatloaf?"

"Sorry. Guess I'm just not hungry."

That night I had the dream again — the old man bumbling around the house, finally coming to the closet and taking out the rod — except this time he walked down the hall and stood in the bedroom door, holding that rod and looking at me. His eyes were squinty like someone who's trying to focus on something a long way off or maybe is real mad. He took a couple of steps towards me and I woke up, all cold and sweaty.

It was just before dawn, kind of gray and nasty-looking

outside, and I ran to the closet. The door was open, and I realized I was standing in something damp. I switched on the light and there, on the rug, was a trail of wet boot prints leading down the hall and out the front door.

I knew what I was supposed to do. I pulled on some clothes, grabbed the rod, vest, waders, and the reel with the silk line, and dashed for the river. I worked the Island Pool for an hour, fishing a little wet fly down and across. With the line tight, it was easier to hook fish, and I landed two. I horsed both trout as hard as I could, almost hoping to break the rod, but it didn't break, and it probably wouldn't have done any good anyway.

That night I slept like a baby and woke up feeling great, but as I walked down the hall on the way to the kitchen I stepped in a wet boot print. I glanced at the closet, but they didn't lead there; they went over to the desk where I'd put the reel. The bottom drawer was open, and the reel was lying on the desk with most of the line stripped off and lying in coils. (I'd forgotten that a silk line is supposed to be stripped off and dried after it's used so it won't rot.) I wiped off the line, hung it on the doorknob, and that evening I greased it with line dressing and put it away.

That was five years ago. Harry got in trouble with the tax people and lost the tackle shop, but he bounced back okay. He's out on the north end of town selling used cars now. In all this time only one strange thing has happened with the rod.

Two winters ago a friend mentioned he'd like to have a little 3-weight rod for winter midge fishing, and I offered to sell him mine. I guess I felt a little uneasy about it, but I needed the money and things had been quiet for months. It was a better rod than he had in mind, but I let him haggle me down pretty good on the price, and he said he'd have the money in a few days.

The next time I saw him he told me he'd been laid off at work, his truck had broken down, and his wife was sick; said he was sorry but he couldn't afford the rod now.

I helped him out a lot that winter, and I guess he thought it was because we were friends. That was part of it, but I also felt guilty. I should have known something like that would happen.

So, I still have the rod. I still don't like it all that much, but I guess I'm finally getting used to it. I haven't had that dream or stepped in any wet footprints in years, but I also make it a point to fish the rod at least once a week between the end of runoff and dove season. To tell you the truth, I'm afraid not to.

CHAPTER SIXTEEN

The Adams Hatch
Part 1 — Getting There

I'M SPEAKING TO YOU
from the cab of a faded-blue, 1970 Chevrolet pickup truck
heading west on I-70 towards Basalt, Colorado and the Frying
Pan River — speaking, that is, into a small tape recorder I
borrowed from a friend's teen-aged daughter. The plan is to
amuse myself and also to determine, once and for all, whether
those insights, ideas, observations, and blasts of Pure Truth we
all get on long, solitary drives are really profound or just the
symptoms of white-line fever. The tape recorder doesn't lie.

I've been staying in the right lane most of the time (the slow
lane where a fourteen-year-old pickup belongs), and I'm being
passed on the left at the moment by an enormous camper, the
kind my lawyer calls a "Wyomingoid road slug." The woman in
the passenger seat (the wife, I assume) is looking at me now with
an expression of undisguised horror.

"Bearded man in a pickup truck talking to himself — and he's got a shotgun in the window rack, too," she seems to be saying to her husband.

The husband looks over and says something. "Oh, I don't think he's dangerous, Martha."

Nice-looking, upper-middle-class couple, probably retired. Somebody's grandma and grandpa. Illinois license plates. Chalk it up to local color, folks, and it's not just a shotgun, it's a Parker. It happens to be dove season here in the Wild West.

I'll have to negotiate with dozens of these four-mile-to-the-gallon land yachts today, but it won't be as bad now as during the regular summer infestation.

So, where was I? Right, an hour from home, having made the right turn at the Point of Geologic Interest parking lot that takes me west, over the Continental Divide, and down into the Colorado River drainage on the Western Slope. That lot is a convenient place to meet fishermen coming out of Denver, and I've spent some time sitting there in the predawn dark and cold, mostly waiting for the legendary Charles K. (Koke) Winter and guzzling coffee from a thermos. You can see Koke coming a long way off even when he doesn't have the john boat on the roof of the car. He's a cabbie and drives with his interior lights burning. For some reason, I've never been moved to go over and see what's so interesting about the geology there, though you can clearly see the stripes in the rock where they blasted a ridge away for the highway.

I enjoy driving alone, especially through beautiful country on the way to a fine trout stream, and with the radio broken. I twisted the tuning knob off last winter in a fit of early-morning impatience and never got around to fixing it. It's okay, since nothing much of value comes through the air anyway. When I'm on the road I like to hear the blues, and they don't play it much anymore. Allow me:

Look on yonder wall
Hand me down my walkin' shoes.

I hear my telephone ringin' (lord, lord)
Sounds like a long distance call

It's a shame you can't hear this and, by the way, what *does* a
long distance call sound like?

As on any trip, I'm experiencing a split consciousness: I'm
here, west of Silver Plume now, heading for the Eisenhower
Tunnel, and I'm also projecting to my destination so much that I
can hear, smell, and see it.

The Frying Pan River and the guy I'll be meeting there (A. K.)
are both old friends, so I pretty much know what to expect: a
whoop and a wave from A. K. when I find him and a river full
of trout and red rocks, down and clear at this time of year. The
hatch (and there *will* be a hatch) will be some small mayfly: the
Blue-winged Olive, maybe the Red Quill, or, if nothing else,
midges. The fish will be hard, but I'll catch some — perhaps not
a lot, but some.

It's after Labor Day and after the famous Green Drake hatch,
so the river and the campgrounds will be more or less deserted,
even though the fishing is every bit as good now as it was earlier
(if not better by virtue of not being elbow to elbow). The nights
will be cold. If the sun stays out, like it is now, the fish will be
spooky and cautious, but the water will have that almost
unbearable crystalline quality it gets in September — freezing
cold and full of light.

When I think of the Pan now, juiced up as I am by
anticipation, I get some precise mental images, complete with
sound and color, geared to my momentary visual attention span:
the 16-inch brookie from two years ago with the pretty burned-
wing Green Drake dry fly in his jaw; Dave Student tying flies on
a kitchen table all but obscured by Miller beer cans; certain
rocks, certain swirls of current.

That's probably because my mind, in spite of itself, has been trained by television, an impression heightened by the fact that the Frying Pan River has *been* on television more than once. It's among the best, and best known, trout streams in the state, and those roving-reporter types at the local stations come up once a year for a story and, one would hope, a fishing trip on the company. It's considered cool — in a no-risk, Gonzo journalism sort of way — to do the story from midstream, in hip boots. They always interview Bill Fitzsimmons, the local hot guide and fishing entrepreneur. In recent years Bill has studiously avoided grinning into the camera and is looking very hard and professional. A famous fisherman.

Bill has a classy fly shop in the town of Basalt — cozy, clean but funky, with Del Canty mounts on the walls and the Pan right out the back door. The last time I checked, I couldn't find a fly in the place that had a barb on the hook.

There's a little-known law in Colorado that every fly shop must have a bird dog on duty during business hours, and that job at Bill's is filled by Tonkin, a Chesapeake Bay retriever so named because as a puppy he went to sleep in a display case full of split-cane rods, inadvertently saving his young life by not chewing them up or peeing on them. Tonkin is the son of old Trapper, not much of a distinction since half the dogs in the county have that curly bronze-colored hair and brown eyes. It's a local tradition.

The place is called "Taylor Creek Angling Services," and you may consider that a blatant plug.

Still, I kind of miss the old place, the one that was actually *on* Taylor Creek. It was a garage-sized cabin where Bill tied the flies he sold, but which may or may not have been open for business in the traditional sense. You could find him there sometimes and were always made welcome, but the feeling you got was somehow not quite like that of a store. If you just strolled in, you always felt like you should have knocked first. If you knocked, you felt a little silly.

Mostly he wasn't there. You'd go over to the house and his

wife, Gerry, would say he was "out on the river someplace," usually with a sport. You'd pass the usual pleasantries while tossing a ten-pound piece of firewood for Trapper, a dog whom it is impossible to ignore even if you wanted to. You were made to feel welcome in the front yard too, even if you were just one of the hundreds of fishermen passing through every year who were so enamored of the scene that they just had to stop by and say hello. On the practical side, news of the hatches, of which there are many, was updated hourly.

It was nice, as, through the passage of time, the way things used to be always seems a little better, but I don't begrudge Bill getting all the yahoos off his front lawn and down in town at the shop. I'm also glad to see him doing well. He's often down in Florida now, fishing for tarpon and bonefish, though he hasn't lost his touch for regular old trout.

There's the Eagle River, the first of either three or four times I'll cross it on this road; I can never remember how many.

As trips go, this one was badly organized and got off to a poor start. A. K. and I had planned to do a week on the Pan like we did last year and the year before. It's developing into a tradition for the month of September, but our schedules didn't mesh, just like they didn't mesh last month when we were supposed to meet Ed Engle down on the Animas River and I ended up going by myself. I remember us wondering then if we weren't getting too busy for our own good and speculating generally about the nature and meaning of success. Is a man who's too busy to go fishing a success? We decided that, in this case, it was a passing inconvenience, but something that needed to be monitored carefully.

A. K. drove over yesterday and will be camped on the Pan

alone for a week. He's one of those people who *can* camp alone for a week, tying flies by lantern light or gazing into the fire and sipping whiskey night after night, happy as an old mossy rock with no particular desire for company. This time *I* was the one who was too busy to spare a week but, in the interest of keeping my priorities realistic, I've stolen an indeterminate number of days anyway. Just making that decision has made my poor overworked heart soar. It's interesting how the power of responsibilities fades in direct relation to the amount of windshield time you put in going in the opposite direction. Errands, creative excuses, and phone calls kept me in and around town until eleven this morning, but if I don't stop to fool around, I'll make the evening rise.

I packed in record time this morning, but looking over at the gear stacked on the seat next to me, it looks like I've got everything: rods, reels, vest, waders, camera, rain gear, warm clothes, and sleeping bag. Anything less essential than that I can bum from A. K. or do without for a few days. Coffee cup? I think so, but I'm not going to stop to check now. The little book with addresses and phone numbers? On the desk at home. To the inevitable question, "where can you be reached?", I answered, "I *can't* be reached." Not entirely true, perhaps, but true enough if that's how I want it.

Just made a pit stop in the thriving metropolis of Eagle, Colorado for gas, oil, and air in the slowly leaking right-front tire, and a cup of what turns out to be really bad coffee. I know from experience that if I try pouring it out the window at 60 miles per hour, I'll get half of it in the face, so I'll just let it sit here and clot.

I guess I shouldn't be sarcastic about Eagle. It's a clean, quiet little burg where you can catch trout and shoot elk more or less right out the back door and where nothing much ever seems to happen. It's not the kind of place the kids stay in once they're out of high school but, to be fair, I'm sure you could get your life just as screwed up there as you could in, say, San Francisco. This is, after all, the last quarter of the Twentieth Century. It's a fine little town; it's just that the coffee is bad.

The Eagle River looks good here — clear — a stream I've somehow never fished, though I hear it's a lot better than most people think. Pretty soon it will get swallowed up in the Colorado which, even at this time of year, will be the color of an old banana daiquiri. We're into that stretch of alternating dirty-gray-colored badlands and crisp red cliffs west of Eagle, east of Gypsum (the same red rock that lines the Frying Pan). Geology again. I don't know anything about it except that it's down there underneath everything, it's meaningful, and it gets exposed by running water and dynamite.

It's not too far to Glenwood Canyon, which is near Glenwood Springs, which is not too far from Basalt. Still a ways to go, but easier to think of in segments. I should make it by four o'clock. I'll stop at Bill's to get the word on the River (he'll say the Adams hatch is on), find out where A. K. is camped in case I miss him on the water, and decompress from the road a little. It should take all of fifteen minutes and is a required stop.

Missing A. K. on the river isn't likely. He'll be at the Picnic Pool or on the Flats, and if I do miss him, I guess I know exactly where he'll be camped. When I find him I'll say, "Are they bitin', mister?" — an old and somewhat obscure private joke.

Here's Glenwood Canyon, one of Colorado's prettiest, seriously marred by the road I'm on now, though less so by the railroad tracks across the river. Still that residual romance of railroads. The road is in the process of being widened into a big, futuristic-looking super highway which is genuinely unattractive and probably environmentally unsound, to boot, though some of the highway department flag women are real pretty — darkly tanned, waving and smiling.

I'm south of Glenwood Springs now, following the Roaring Fork River up to its confluence with the Frying Pan at Basalt, feeling a distinct lack of guilt at playing hookey. As I said, A. K. will be up here for a week, catching trout, frying beans on the fire, and speaking nary a word out loud, but in a day or so I'll begin to feel that vague gravitational pull that means I'd better get back. There are deadlines to meet, money to be made after all, and, if the truth be known, there's this lady law student with long black hair. She's not entirely sure she wants to get involved with me; however, it occurs to me that our relative positions when we had that conversation last night might indicate that we're already "involved" in some sense.

Be that as it may, at the moment there's nowhere I'd rather be than driving six miles per hour over the speed limit (about all the old truck can muster without shaking apart) down Highway 80 towards the Frying Pan, going fishing in spite of everything. One is tempted to speculate here on the meaning of life, but why bother? Oil pressure's good, battery charging, half tank of gas.

Nearly there now, and things are getting more familiar. There's the bridge where you can put a boat in, and right up here is the hole where A. K., Dave Student, and I caught all the whitefish that time. We were up here in April staying in one of Bill's cabins, and the fishing on the Pan was unusually lousy. After two days we came down here to the Roaring Fork, caught a mess of firm, cold-water whitefish, went back to the cabin, and made a huge pot of Chippino, a strong Italian fish stew designed to mask the taste of marginal seafood. Bill said the cabin stank of it for weeks afterwards.

Part 2: Leave My Mother Out of This

I found A. K.'s pickup parked at the Flats under the dam, the only car in sight. It was half past four, just right. I rigged up slowly and carefully, deliberately not rushing — the equivalent of taking a few deep breaths to relax. A trout stream should be approached with a degree of reverence, for practical as well as aesthetic reasons: if you jump out of the truck after five hours on the road and hop into the stream, you'll not only wade right through a pod of rising trout, but will probably fall down and get your ass wet, too. Be calm — you're there. Squint at the sky, sniff the air, listen to the water. Tell yourself there's no rush, even if there is.

A. K. had seen me drive up and was coming down the far bank. I waded out to meet him with my flyless leader held against the cork grip. With some streams I'm confident enough to tie on an Adams before stepping into the water, but the Pan isn't one of them. There's too much to be wrong about. I could have put on a Blue-winged Olive dry or the emerger and been making a reasonable bet, but tying a fly on the tippet is the kind of commitment that needs to be honored for an appropriate amount of time. For one thing, you don't want to appear flighty and indecisive, even to yourself. For another, furiously changing flies is a sign of panic, and fishermen in a state of hysteria seldom catch trout. It's best to wait, even though wading a stream with no fly on the leader is a little like deer hunting with an unloaded rifle.

A. K. and I met in the middle of the ankle-deep ford. We did not shake hands. That ceremony is reserved for more unique occasions than convening on a trout stream. "Are they bitin', mister?" I asked. "As a matter of fact, yes," he said, though apparently not at the moment, or he wouldn't have come to meet me.

The word was Blue-winged Olives (ah-ha!) mixed with some little Red Quills, some midges, and the odd caddis fly, blending into a mixed fall of spinners — a drawn-out, sparse, multiple-hatch situation not atypical of this water. A. K. had also taken some fish, including a 20-inch cutt/bow, on a #12 March Brown and had seen a few of the big mayflies. That wasn't surprising, though there's some debate about exactly what this bug is.

For all practical purposes, the Green Drake emergence was over, the famous banker's hours hatch, starting predictably at ten o'clock in the morning and lasting till three o'clock in the afternoon, the one that seems to be attended by half the fly-fishers in the state. But even weeks after the major hatch, one can still pound up fish using the Drake pattern, presumably because trout remember the big mayflies and also because there are continued, sporadic appearances of a big fly that some consider to be a residual Green Drake and that others confidently refer to as the Great Slate-winged Red Quill.

To my eye, the later flies are identical to the Green Drakes except that they're noticeably lighter in color and have a faint rusty instead of grayish green cast to them. It's also significant that the March Brown produces a bit better than the standard Green Drake tie. A #12 Adams has been known to work also on both hatches.

Be that as it may, I guess I'm only mildly interested in whether this later fly is the real Green Drake or a different insect, my only firm opinion being that "March Brown" trips off the tongue more lightly than "Great Slate-winged Red Quill," a considerable handle for what anyone but a fly-fisherman would call a brown bug. It *is* a nice little secret, though, both the obscure, late hatch and the lighter pattern. It's what anglers are ultimately after — a shred of understanding with a practical application.

So, the latest word on current conditions. This is one of the advantages of showing up a day late.

Nothing much was happening on the Flats (there were two

guys drifting big caddis dries over a pod of three or four trout who were clearly taking midges) so we worked our way downstream. There were some fish working in the Gauging Station Pool as well as some in the braided water downstream. A. K. said he'd taken his 20-incher and seen some other good trout in the pocket water below the channel and so, understandably, headed off in that direction, trailing plumes of pipe smoke that hung in the still, cool air.

I stood at the Gauging Station watching trout rise with a lazy but deliberate head-and-tail roll, fingering the zipper on my vest, beneath which reposed a whole box of Adamses, sizes 10 through 20. The Pan has the reputation of being a persnickety, match-the-hatch-or-else kind of stream, and it *is* that, though you can still find codgers fishing with Phillipson or Granger rods, sometimes fitted with ten-dollar automatic reels, taking trout hand over fish with a #12 Humpy. I've conducted some serious business on nearly half a dozen mayfly hatches here using an Adams in the right size (Bill is only half joking when he talks about the Adams hatch) but have just as often spent the evening tying Blue Duns with lighter bodies and darker wings than the ones that didn't quite click that day. It's a stream that can teach you about the frailty of your beliefs.

I tied on an Adams, size 20.

It became obvious in a few minutes that this was one of those times. The fish showed some interest, doing bumps and short inspection rises, but not taking, something you see more often on a heavily fished stream than on a wilder one where, when a trout moves for a fly, he usually hits it. Trout who get fished for often develop the capacity to commit in a considered way, allowing for a last-minute change of mind.

Okay. It's probably the spinner. A quick look into the current at my feet revealed a good number of them, mixed with the last scattered duns of the Olive hatch and the odd little Red Quill. I should have known that, *did* in fact know it, but the belief that trout aren't really all that selective needs to be hauled out and tried by way of an observance.

The religious symbol of this belief is the Adams dry fly. It's a pretty thing, with its mixed hackle and grizzly wings, the universal favorite of all but the most exacting fly-fishers. The pattern was originally tied as a caddis by Len Halliday on Michigan's Boardman River but has since gone far beyond that to straddle the line in the minds of anglers between the imitative fly and the attractor. It looks a little like everything, not exactly like anything, and seems to have great totemic power. Pinned to the wall above A. K.'s fly-tying bench is a slightly out-of-focus snapshot of a rather ordinary-looking piece of water, not worth a second glance until you learn that it's the famous Adams pool where the fly was first fished, at which point it becomes a kind of icon.

In fact, the Adams is symbolic of fly-fishing itself, a sport that, at its best, mixes the basics of science with dark powers on one hand and bumbling luck on the other. It's a good pattern for fishermen who catch trout by suspending belief in any particular system and who don't feel driven to know everything. It's a cowboy's fly, notwithstanding that it comes from Michigan. For that matter, so do pickup trucks.

Between clipping off the Adams (a little sadly) and replacing it with a #18 Rusty Spinner, I glanced downstream to where A. K. was holding a deeply bowed and nicely throbbing rod, the only sign of his excitement being the shorter, faster puffs of smoke from the pipe. Very pretty.

It occurred to me that I was standing in exactly the spot I was standing in several years ago in April when I mistook a bear for Koke Winter. We'd separated on the river and I had slogged down to the Gauging Station through the deep, crusty snow to fish a nymph. After a troutless hour, I heard footsteps crunching through the snow behind me. As far as I knew we were the only two fishermen out that day (a cold and dreary afternoon in

midweek) so I said over my shoulder,
"Doing any good, Koke?"
"Grunt."
"Uh . . . Koke?"

It was a little cinnamon-colored black bear — I remember him as kind of pretty, now that he's not breathing down my neck. We were both terrified, but he ran up a scree slope while I stood where I was, somehow maintaining control of my bladder. I'd have jumped in the river if I'd thought of it.

Not a big deal, of course, the kind of thing fishermen get used to. Later I simply mentioned to Koke that I'd seen a bear, though I had the unreasonable suspicion (the same one you'd have if you knew him) that he'd somehow staged the whole thing.

I shook myself out of this reverie, incidentally glancing over my shoulder, and cast the spinner to a steadily rising trout just on the near side of the fast current. He took, I set, and suddenly, finally, I was fishing. Just fishing. The roar of wind from the open truck window was replaced by the liquid roar of the stream, and all concern for money, women and other personal demons was gone. Of course it was the spinner fall. I just hadn't been paying attention.

In camp that evening A. K. was orchestrating supper and drinks while I built the fire and admired the setup. He'd picked a spot near a little creek, for the music at night, he said, and also to cool the beer. The tent was next to the picnic table, on which sat the venerable old Michigan camp kitchen. This thing is a large, well-built pine box that can be padlocked shut and also bicycle-chained to a tree. The side folds down to form a working surface and to reveal a Coleman stove, pots and pans, staples and spices, coffeepot, and a bar consisting of a bottle of Canadian Club and some tin cups, all set securely in their own cubicles.

Inside the tent was A. K.'s air mattress and sleeping bag, and on the other side of the entrance sat a chair and table for tying flies. There was a lantern for light. Just outside, a bare tree held a set of wader hangers. A. K. belongs to the base-camp school of living outside. His camps are there for a reason (usually fishing) and the implied motto is, "suffer if you must, but not if you don't have to."

We were in the big campground above the dam, alone but for one other camper down closer to the reservoir. In another week the iron gate with the "closed for the season" sign would be swung across the entrance, and soon thereafter the place would begin to slowly and quietly fill up with snow. Grounds like this are worse than towns in the summer, but in the off season they're nicely deserted, eliciting the same kind of pleasant loneliness as a single ranch yard light burning across otherwise empty country at three in the morning. In September the deer start coming down at night.

It was empty enough that when two guys in a well-used old van pulled in near us, we gave the casual howdy-there-pilgrim wave, basically unoffended by the company. They were grouse hunters, maybe, or even fellow anglers, though the latter was doubtful, as they didn't come over to ask about the fishing.

Since they didn't start playing rock and roll, we promptly forgot about them, stuffed ourselves with beef stew, wheat bread, and canned peaches, and settled down to poking the fire and rambling. Two hours and several drinks later, we were reliving the time when we were marginally stumped by a mayfly hatch, a season or two ago on this very river, and spent the better part of an evening at our respective fly-tying travel kits reinventing the Quill Gordon.

Then we noticed the sounds of a scuffle coming from the van — thumps, grunts, muffled profanities. We carried our drinks over for a closer look and a better listen. It may have been in our minds to try to break it up if that seemed appropriate, though we'd both have dived into the bushes if knives, axes, or shotguns became part of the deal.

There was obviously a fistfight going on in the van (it even rocked on its springs a time or two), and during one lull in the action, we clearly heard one of the contestants say, "You leave my mother out of this, you (deleted)."

Things then quieted down to a low grumbling argument that sounded plenty combative but essentially harmless. A. K. and I decided this was not something we cared to get involved in or even learn any more about. The world, we agreed, is certainly full of trouble.

The next morning, I awoke to the sound of A. K. wrestling into his clothes while sitting on his sleeping bag. This awkward performance is a holdover from past days; the new tent is tall enough to stand up in, but it will take a few seasons for that to sink in. At first it seemed to be pitch dark beyond the tent flap, but a second look through more open eyes revealed a faint, cold, rosy glow along the horizon.

This is the only part of camping with A. K. I don't enjoy. He's one of those guys who spring to their feet an hour before dawn, happy, hungry, cheerful, exuberant, and minus a hangover. "Good morning," he'll shout, "you gonna lay there all day or you gonna go fishing?" It's enough to make you puke, but at least the coffee's ready when I drag myself out into the open, trailing untied bootlaces, blinking at the last frigid stars.

Coffee, breakfast, sandwiches for lunch, and the squaring away of camp were accomplished in a typically unhurried but brisk way. One does not dawdle around camp when there are trout to be caught. During these chores the van pulled past us and headed up the road. A. K. swore there was only one person in it, so I walked over to their spot to see if there was a body. Dealing with a murder would have killed at least a half day's fishing, but I supposed one did have certain civic duties. There was no corpse, though I'll admit to not looking under every bush.

On the water, A. K. wanted the Picnic Pool, while I decided on the long run upstream — there were trout rising all over the place. In that last moment before splitting up, when some words of encouragement are considered proper, A. K. turned to me and said, "By the way, leave my mother out of this."

This is how crazy old coots evolve. Leaving mother out of it will join "Are they bitin', mister?" and other vague allusions and mispronunciations — like sounding the "P" in Pflueger — taking us one step closer to the point where people will begin to wonder just what the hell we're giggling about.

There were scattered small mayflies on the water (surely the Olives) and a few ubiquitous midges. The trout were working in the current — hungry, eager. With supreme confidence, I tied on a #20 Adams.

CHAPTER SEVENTEEN

Night-fishing

THE GIRL SINGER ON
the late-night television show is a knockout — busty, willowy, all
but coming out of her dress as she giggles and bounces around
in her chair. The kind of woman that, as near as I can
determine, does not actually exist. I'm beginning to lose interest.

"I understand you have a concert tour coming up."

"That's right, Johnny . . . ."

And that's all I can take.

I turn off the set, down the last of a cup of strong coffee, grab
my hat, and go for the door. Out in the darkness the gear is
already stowed in the pickup, which is aimed in the right
direction. With my hand on the doorknob, I turn and tell the
dog to stay. He opens one eye and looks at me as if to say,
"And where would I be going at this time of night?" or maybe,
"You never take me anywhere. You don't love me." It's hard to
tell.

Five minutes later I'm parked off the road above the lake and am rigging up in the headlights, after which I have to wait another five minutes or so for my eyes to get used to the dark. There's a light across the lake, and I try to picture the fisherman dozing in a lawn chair with his lantern resting on the beer cooler, waiting for a catfish to pick up his golf-ball-sized gob of worms or, if he's a purist, aged chicken guts. Fun.

Then again, what the hell. He's not hurting anything, and if I have to change flies, I can silhouette the eye of the hook against his light rather than blind myself with the flashlight. If there's a trick to night-fishing, it's to get into the darkness, although, having said that, I'll have to admit to carrying not one, but two lights: a little AA battery job that I can hold in my mouth, leaving my hands free for unavoidable chores, and a great big bright sucker for finding the truck again and for determining quickly whether that big, vague, heavily breathing shape in the darkness is a cow or a grizzly bear. There hasn't been a grizzly around here in a hundred years but, in the middle of the night, one likes to make sure.

My gear is spartan and stout, well thought out. There are the two flashlights (the little one in a breast pocket, the big one clipped to the belt), a pair of toenail clippers in the right pants pocket, and a sheepskin hatband full of flies — poppers on one side, streamers on the other. No fly is smaller than a size 4. I'm after bass.

The rod is a heavy 9-foot split cane with an 8-weight forward line. I'm not using a cane rod to impress anyone (I would, but no one is going to *see* me); I'm using it because this particular one is slow and heavy and I can feel my backcast, a distinct advantage when you can't see what you're doing. It's also long enough to keep the big flies with their deeply gapped, lethal hooks away from my head.

The whole thing is a model of efficiency, which only illustrates that I don't do this very often and am not very good at it. It's eleven-thirty, too early, but if I'd stayed home any longer I'd have had to have a drink or two, and night-fishing is problematic enough when sober.

It's a warm, clear night, moonless but with stars. I can see the lake as the near edge of a purplish disk and can make out the closer cattails. I know from having fished here for six or seven years in daylight — and a handful of times at night — that I can go down to the water at the sandy place and cast to my left up against the cattails. I'll work a wedge-shaped piece of water twice or three times before I move down the bank a little, pushing the wedge ahead of me (and will naturally drop that plan at the sound of a splash or the spreading rings of a heavy swirl in the starlight). I'm wearing only hip boots to keep me from wading too deep. The idea is to work the shallows where, presumably, the big fish will be.

Night-fishing can be a pain in the ass, literally and figuratively, because you can't see where you're going or what you're doing. I refuse to night-fish water I'm not familiar with by daylight, but even so, stumps and barbed-wire fences change position and the drop-offs creep in closer to shore. The whole place seems different, and you find yourself doing things that are analogous to getting up in the middle of the night to go to the bathroom and ending up in the hall closet. I always feel like I'm very close to, as they say, "stumbling around in the dark." It goes without saying that the blackest nights are the best for fishing.

There are some things you can do to simplify the situation. You can keep your gear to a bare minimum to reduce the amount of fumbling, and you can plan routes to and from the water that keep you away from known pitfalls like forgotten fences shrouded in vegetation, sinkholes, deadfalls, and all those other things you lightly and casually step around when you can see them. On this lake I'll go in at the sandy spot, wade north along the cattail bank (where the bottom is mucky but of uniform depth), get out at the far end where the cattails give way to high grass over firm ground, swing up to the road, and back to the truck. If I'm not ready to bag it at that point, I can go on up the north bank, which is open, sloping, and less interesting but sometimes productive anyway. This particular spot is a piece of cake, comparatively, and I can probably do the whole thing without using a flashlight unless I get spooked or take a bass I just have to get a look at.

The preparations — scouting and gearing up — are essentially intellectual pursuits, the kind of thing that can look good on paper. At some point, however, you're faced with actually going out there, and that takes some getting used to.

For one thing, the hours are freaky, so much so that in some circles "night-fishing" is a euphemism for catting around. What we're talking about here is the kind of night-fishing you do with a fly rod, and the best time is in the darkest, quietest hours between midnight and false dawn. Going fishing at midnight and coming back before sunrise doesn't easily fit into many schedules, and that may be what keeps so many fishermen away from it.

Something else that discourages would-be night-fishers is a basic fear of the dark. This comes in two overlapping varieties: the fairly rational dislike of operating blind (the fear of real physical injury) and that deeper, darker thing that made our ancestors get into fire in the first place and which has made bats symbols of evil instead of, say, bluebirds.

Now, I know in my mind there's nothing out there that will hurt me. What's abroad at night? Rabbits, mice, voles, foxes, coyotes, owls, house cats, deer, bats, frogs, and all manner of insects, including mosquitos, which aren't especially pleasant but are far from sinister. Bats can be spooky at times, but they're actually kind of cute. The only dangerous animals around here are the rattlesnakes, and even the balmiest summer nights are too cool for them.

It's really lovely out there at night, pleasantly cool after the hot, dry days, and blissfully quiet. There is, of course, no real silence in nature, only layer after layer of softer sounds: the rustlings, ploppings, and buzzings of God knows what, the sighing of the air and the water, punctuated now and then by the

bark of a farm dog in the distance, the unearthly yowling of
coyotes, or the muttering of a lonesome duck with insomnia. It's
peaceful, and if I happen to get scared, I always have the big
flashlight hanging on my hip like a .44 magnum. Ultimately the
fear is a little thing, a subtle spice without which the experience
would be just fine but still not quite as good. We human beings
don't belong out on the water at night any more than we belong
in space, but we go anyway, just because.

Well, just because the big fish feed at night — the largemouth
bass, the brown trout, and some others, too — I usually fish for
bass in the evenings, expecting, and often finding, a flurry of
activity in the hour or so between sunset and actual nightfall.
That's a transition zone, as real as the one between deep and
shallow water, and the fish like it, regardless of the biological
reasons. They come in and charge around, bigger fish than
during the day, taking bigger flies.

That's the closest to night-fishing most fishermen get: staying
on the water until it's dark. But as night comes on they notice
that things slow down and it gets cool, and they're tired and a
little hungry. You know, the energy fades and it's time to go.
You could use a drink and, anyway, it's *dark*.

Things do slow down early in the night but, the way I figure
it, about the time I'm ready to turn on the tube and see who the
latest girl singer with the obvious charms and doubtful talent is,
the big bass are just beginning to nose up into the shallows.
These are the fish that are as much as twice the size of the best
ones you'll take there during the day (in the case of my local
bass lake), maybe as heavy as 6 or 8 pounds. In better water,
who knows.

It's an article of faith among fishermen that any body of
healthy water holds some monsters, fish that no one ever catches
but that are, nonetheless, there. In most cases, this faith is
justified. These are the bass that loom out of the darkness at
three o'clock in the morning looking for mice, frogs, baby
muskrats, and 2/0 bass poppers. Any fisheries biologist will tell

you they're there, though the information will likely be couched in terms of statistical anomalies, meaning there aren't a lot of them. Their dietary preferences seem shocking on one hand, but we do not laugh at the flies tied to imitate such things, and bass flytiers are in a constant unspoken competition to see who can tie the most adorable mouse.

All fishermen know this: that the biggest bass eat (or would prefer to eat) food organisms just below those favored by alligators, i.e., dogs and small children. Just look at the fish. He's designed to take the biggest mouthful possible. The gape of his jaws roughly equals the circumference of his body. Fishermen also know the lore of night-fishing, but most of them still ignore it.

The whole night-fishing for bass procedure was impressed on me early in life by my Uncle Leonard. I remember the first time we went out at night (it may have been the first time I had *ever* gone out at night). The fish were enormous, though certain details, like Uncle Leonard's turning the car lights out when we turned off the main road and his telling me to be quiet so we didn't scare the fish while we were still half a mile from the pond, make me suspect now that we might have been poaching. Night-fishing is not only a way to get at the bigger fish, in some circles it's also a way to keep from getting caught. In my youth I was led to believe that only dilettantes and outright chickens fished for bass in daylight.

Night-fishing isn't something a lot of us get into seriously. It takes the kind of dedication to actually catching fish that many of us don't have; but it should be done from time to time, if for no other reason than that it's *there* to be done — an easy adventure. If you ignore too many things like that, you'll eventually end up with a general dissatisfaction with your life. You'll go sour and won't know why. It will be because you never fished at night.

Tonight I'm using a standard night fly. It has a heavy black fur tail (dyed rabbit in this case, though it could be anything) and a body of tightly palmered black hackle, maybe six or eight feathers wrapped on the shank of a #2 stinger hook. It looks like a bottle brush with a fuzzy handle and, with the addition of some rubber legs, might pass for an all-black version of the French Tickler streamer Russ Kipp designed for Montana's Beaver Head River. With hackle-point tails it would be a Marsh Hare. I call it the Night Fly, having temporarily run out of better names.

Night flies are traditionally black, or at least dark in color, and heavily dressed, the idea being that dark colors produce sharper silhouettes against the night sky and that the heavy dressings make more noise as well as increase visibility. Noise-making is an accepted function of surface bugs but it's often ignored in the design of streamers. A lot of the old-timey bass streamers, and some for trout, too, had gold or silver spinner blades attached to the front ends. This was apparently done to add flash, but it also made the flies run louder. Putting propellers on my night streamers is among the things I'm meaning to try but have yet to get around to.

My only other standard night fly is the classic Arbogast flyrod Hula Popper, the black one. I fish a #2, the biggest they make, even though they're a little hard to cast on anything short of a 9-weight, weight-forward line. This fly (or "lure," if you prefer) is the loudest of the hard-bodied poppers, much louder than any struggling mouse or swimming frog. In fact, the sound it makes is more like the chugging strike of a big bass, and I think it attracts fish by mimicking feeding activity. Think of it as a bass call. Lately I've taken to removing the rubber skirts from these things and replacing them with long feather tails and hackles. They look a bit more traditional that way and may even be a little easier to cast.

Many other things will work, of course, and if you go out at night only occasionally you don't have to develop a whole new set of patterns for it. Still, this big black fly business is part of the mythology of night-fishing, a strange and solitary sport in which even the fish remain mythological most of the time. If the truth were known, even the truly serious night-fishers don't haul in enormous bass on a regular basis, and those of us who only dabble in it hear and feel them rarely, landing them almost never.

Tonight I'm fishing the streamer in the interest of efficiency. Striking by sound, as you have to do with a popper, is too much like playing chess without looking at the board — something best left to those who actually know what they're doing. A streamer is fished on a tight line, enabling you to feel the strike, so your only problem is casting the thing.

In front of me now is a stretch of relatively open shallow bottom immediately adjacent to deep water bordered on the dry-land side by a narrow cattail marsh populated by frogs, mice, snakes, fingerling bass, crappies, and bluegills, as well as golden chubs. Most of these feed on insects, some of which are predatory, feeding on other insects who, in their turn, exist on vegetation or zooplankton, which, somewhere down in the elusive depths of creation, generate life from mud, water, and sunlight. Or at least that's how I understand it. I'm here doing my level best to complete the food chain by taking a fish so big and so far up the system that he has no enemies except me and the guy across the lake in the lawn chair, who is probably deeply asleep and dreaming by now. If he's good he has a little tin bell on his rod tip to alert him to the fact that the battle has begun.

If I do connect tonight, my place in the food chain will probably be symbolic, as I'll almost surely release the fish. I have sworn to kill, stuff, and mount any bass approaching 10 pounds caught fairly on a fly rod anywhere in the state of Colorado, even if I have to mortgage the truck to pay for it, but it's highly unlikely that I'll get called on that, and to just *eat* a statistical anomaly is probably sinful.

I'm casting up close to the cattails, which reveal themselves as a taller, more substantial darkness. The water there is less than two feet deep. A bass could be cruising the edge or even back in there, swimming among the stalks. Once, in late evening light, I spotted a big largemouth by the movements of the weeds as he shouldered his way through them lazily, maybe eating damselfly nymphs or looking for something bigger. I cast a deer-hair froggie with spots and eyeballs to a little open patch of water he was headed for, jiggled it once just as he got there, and he swallowed it with a heart-rending burble. For once it was a bass and not a muskrat, and I felt like Dave Whitlock. But tonight I can see nothing, and imagining you can *hear* a bass moving the cattails is a good way to give yourself the screaming willies.

I'm looking hard, though there's little to see, and am listening anyway. Whether or not I want to hear the heavy splash of a strike to anything besides my streamer is debatable. I'd cast to it, but it could be a huge bass who has just consumed a quarter of his weight in raw bullfrog and is, consequently, not all that hungry anymore. For that matter, it could be a beaver. I'd cast to it anyway.

The fly is only lightly weighted, enough to get it under the surface but not enough to slam it to the bottom or ruin its action. It's so quiet I can hear the blip as it hits the water. I wait until I think it has sunk a few inches (during which time a fish could hit it, so I strain to listen, tightening my scalp muscles, as if that would help) and then begin the retrieval with a hard pull. I imgine the sound it must make: "voooooop." A 2-foot-long bass has heard this through his sensitive lateral line. Safely covered by darkness, he ponderously waves his tail and approaches the victim silently, hideous jaws already opening. Then again, maybe not. There is no strike on this cast nor on the next twenty.

Sometime later there is a tug on the line when I strip it and, though I thought I was relaxed, I set the hook too fast and way too hard. The gob of weeds comes loose reluctantly, by the roots, and when I clean the hook I notice that the water is almost exactly the same temperature as the air. The only way I know my hand is in it is by the slight liquid resistance.

I think this could be the wrong night. Intense night-fishers figure the phase of the moon, the barometer, and all kinds of other great movements, the proper combination of which will bring the bass of local legend to their feet like puppies. For me it's the dark of the moon and nothing much to get up for the following morning, period. Then, on the water, ignorance settles on me like a fleet of leeches. It occurs to me that all the bars are closed.

Half an hour later (intuitive time) it actually happens. I let the fly sink and when I begin to strip it in, there's a moving weight attached. I set the hook smartly, feel a ponderous wiggle, and cinch it once more to sink the point to the bend. The fish runs slowly for open water and turns grudgingly against the palmed reel.

Turning him out there was a stupid move. In the open water he would only pick up those flimsy weeds that aren't enough to break my short, 17-pound test leader. I'd have cranked him in as an almost dead weight and peeled him out of the crap like a banana. Now he's going for the stout tangles in shallow water, where I will lose him.

I'm sidestepping slowly but frantically out away from shore, and the water that slips into my hip boots cannot be the same water that seemed so warm before. The rod is above my head, in both hands. I imagine I can feel the molecular structure that holds the linear cells of the bamboo together giving way, atom by atom, bringing closer by the second the day when this already thirty-year-old rod will become a useless noodle. I'm playing this fish like an idiot but can't come up with anything better. I catch myself thinking about a friend who used to drive a garbage truck for a company known as BF&I. "What's that mean?", I asked him once. "Brute Force & Ignorance," he said.

A few yards from the cattails the fish turns, miraculously. Not miraculously, I realize. If he was as big as I want him to be, he would *not* have turned. Still a good fish, but, suddenly, it gets easier.

I hand land him by the lower jaw and shine the big light on him: stubby, fat, glassy-eyed. I think, 5 pounds, so let's say 4½ — but then, thinking of all those magazine articles, I stick my fist in his mouth, and it fits. So let's go ahead and say 5. For this water, a hell of a bass.

A friend who lives nearby would consider it proper to be awakened at this hour to have a 5-pound bass flopped on his kitchen table. He would produce a couple of cold beers and his wife, being a sport herself, would be of good cheer.

But by morning it would pale to a "nice fish," which is exactly what it is, and the bastard would probably get out the scale. The bass I want would be worth waking up the whole town for and would establish me forever as mucho hombre, the man who is *out there* while the rest of them are safe in their little beds.

When I release the fish he bumps my leg once in his confusion before he is irretrievably gone.

CHAPTER EIGHTEEN

Cutthroat Pilgrimage

THE LAKES ARE SMALL,
rocky bottomed, cold, scattered blue spots on the topographical
maps, lying in a north-south band up near the Continental
Divide. Most are named, but a surprising number remain
anonymous.

There are brook trout here, some rainbows, even a few
browns at the relatively lower altitudes, but the romance lies
with the cutthroats. Just the sound of the word suggests the wild
and untouched. "You get far enough up on the Middle Fork and
you start running into cutthroats." Hearing that, you can smell
the refrigerated air coming off the snowfields and hear the lazy
honking of ravens, the implication being that the place where
you start running into cutthroats is too far into the backcountry
for the lazy or fainthearted. That's not always the case, but it's a
nice thought.

One June, to no clear purpose, but on something slightly more
substantial than a whim, I walked to the top of Niwot Ridge for

a view of the lake country. It was appropriately mystical.
Standing on the spine of the Continental Divide, I urinated into
the drainages of two oceans more or less simultaneously (a little
childish, maybe, but a required ritual) and then perched on a
flat rock that would be the ideal vantage point for someone who
decided to just sit and watch the universe run down.

I chose that particular hill because it's the easiest place in the
area to achieve the Divide on foot and because it's a walk
instead of a climb — long, gruelling, tedious, but still a walk.
My early flirtation with real climbing ended suddenly some years
ago when I learned, by way of one of those horrible, life-jolting,
late-night phone calls, that the man who'd been teaching me had
fallen to his death. That call was among the things that have
made me a more serious and dedicated fisherman, a sport in
which life and limb can be risked on an occasional and usually
voluntary, rather than a regular, basis.

On a long, trudging hike to 11,000 feet above sea level, one
finds things to think about: that, for instance, Niwot, for whom
the mountain is named, was an important Indian hereabouts
back in the old days when Haystack Mountain was known as
Peckers Knob and when other things were also still as they
should be. The word means "left hand" and left-handedness
was considered by the Indians to be very big medicine. I
dismissed as idle the thought that I was righthanded and didn't
have a mountain named after me. As I said, it was a long walk.

This area hides approximately sixty lakes. I say
"approximately" because I've never bothered to count them and
because I try to ignore the artificial boundaries where a national
park becomes wilderness area and where a wilderness area
becomes national forest, so I wouldn't know where to stop
counting if I ever got started. There's also the problem of
definition. The majority of these are cutthroat lakes, some hold
other species or a mix (cutts and brookies is my favorite
combination), and a few are devoid of fish for one reason or
another. Whatever the cartographers say, a body of still water

that doesn't hold trout isn't a lake, it's a pothole. After fifteen
years in the area, I still haven't determined which is which in all
cases, though I will if my legs hold out.

At first I was disappointed that I couldn't see more water
from the hard-won summit of Niwot Ridge. I expected the
whole thing to be laid out for me, but then I realized that that's
possible only when viewed from the air or the implied aerial
view of maps. After a little while the idea that the lakes were
lying hidden in the trees, over the far ridges, and hanging in
cirques began to appeal to me. It was either that or climb a
higher mountain. The few I *could* see were enough and, after all,
a lake is only truly meaningful when your backpack and rod case
are lying on its bank.

Fishing these high cutthroat lakes can be about as problematic
as fly-fishing gets, though in a different way than some of us are
used to. At the highest altitudes, the fishing season — that
period of time between ice-out and the first winter storms —
can be as short as six weeks. Farther down the slope things start
earlier and last later, but it's still easy to get blown out on either
end, especially when you have to hike in some distance.

Some friends and I have tried to deal with this by developing
the concept of the test lake. Test lakes have the virtue of being
easily accessible by road or short trail while at the same time
being at roughly the same altitude and on the same slope as
more remote ones. In many cases the test lakes hold brookies or
stocked rainbows, while the ones deeper into the country harbor
cutthroats, but otherwise they're comparable. Rather than make
a completely wild guess, you can drive up to, say Sprague Lake
and if the ice is off there, you can figure it's off old Lost Lake
too.

This isn't exactly a foolproof procedure, but it beats basing an
expedition into the high country in the early summer on nothing
more than the fact that you're, by God, ready to catch some
cutthroats. It's an attempt at understanding — which is what
fishing in general is — but, like fishing, the test lake theory

allows for its misadventures.

If you hit a good high-country cutthroat lake within a few weeks of ice-out, you may find yourself in the midst of some of the easiest fishing you'll ever see, incredibly easy compared to normal cutthroat fishing. If you hit it just right, the trout are as hungry as spring bears and haven't yet begun to spawn. If they *are* on the beds, you take one or two, just to have a look at them, and then force yourself to leave them alone. Sometimes the fish are a bit skinny and a little weak from the long winter under the ice. At times you'll play a nice one too long and release him with the small, gnawing suspicion that you've done him in. Even the gentle art of fly-fishing has it's little moments of tragedy.

Maybe you quit then because you don't quite feel right about taking unfair advantage and because the catching is too easy to be proud of. The victory here isn't landing fish so much as it is arriving at the lake at *the moment* through the exercise of (you tell yourself) your considerable steely-eyed, wood-smoke wisdom. With trout still rising, you can assemble a twig fire, brew a pot of coffee to cut the still wintry-feeling chill, tell yourself, "I am one smart s.o.b. and kindhearted, to boot," and sit there reveling in self-righteousness. At these rare times I typically dismiss the thought that an angler who has reached the highest levels of enlightenment might be tempted to leave the fishing tackle at home and just go up to have a look. As it stands now, though, I'm a fisherman, not a saint. You can ask anyone.

In any event, occasions for that kind of self-congratulation are not to be passed up and so, once or twice every spring, when anyone with the brains they were born with is down at the farm ponds catching bedding bluegills or bass, a few of us scope out the appropriate test lake and then slog into the high country in search of the first cutthroats. The self-congratulation is well earned when you figure that out of two trips every spring, you hit it right once every other season.

Last May A. K. and I decided to try it on Little So-and-So

Lake, which is just east and a little downhill from *Big* So-and-So Lake. It had been a heavy snow year, with the lowland streams deep in muddy runoff. Even the road up to the trailhead parking lot was closed, adding a round trip of about three miles to an already healthy day hike.

We pushed it hard, the usual trail chatter degenerating into concentrated silence as we alternately swung along and waded the drifts. There was too much snow to walk in, but not enough for snowshoes or skis. There was also enough of the crusty white stuff to obscure the trail, and we walked right off it when it made the ninety-degree turn to the northwest.

It was about an hour later when A. K. stopped in his tracks, looked around, and said, "This doesn't look right. This slope is too steep. And see that ridge? That's supposed to be a lot closer."

True enough. This, as we agreed later, is the rather significant difference between being lost and just "sort of turned around."

We agreed on the proper direction and picked a slope that looked like it would be easy going. Less than half a mile to the north, we topped out on a shelf we took to be on the level with our destination and found ourselves standing on the bank of a new and strange little lake. It was a lovely thing, maybe two or three acres, roughly round, sitting in a little basin with a steep pitch on the west side and heavy spruce and fir woods around it. Another hundred yards to the east and we'd have strolled right past it. A single trout rose against the north bank.

Blinded by our original plan, we carefully noted the lake's location (south of that, just under this) and headed on to where we were going.

We arrived at the second lake instead of the first but, since they're only a little ways apart, we declared it a direct hit. By now it was drizzling, the wind was up, and the air temperature had dropped into the forties. As it turned out, it didn't matter which lake we found because both were free of ice but dead, in that monumental way the high lakes have, as if the trout had all slipped into another dimension. The water in both lakes was stinging cold and sizzling in what became a steady rain. Considering our ration of daylight and the absence of fish, we cased our rods and hiked out, reexperiencing the fact that wading through snow is only a little easier going downhill than up.

Back at the truck (finally) we drank warmish coffee from a thermos and dripped and steamed as the heater took hold. Whipped. We were forced, as fishermen often are, into a poetic interpretation of events: it had been beautiful, lonely, wild, not another human footprint, but some of a mountain lion.

It was about then that a red sports car with New York plates arrived, spilling heavy-metal rock and roll into the wet air, drowning out the pounding of rain on the roof of the pickup (one of the finest of sounds). Two college-aged boys hopped out and began passing an enormous joint back and forth. "Far *out*," one of them said, "get a load of *this*."

It was clearly time to leave. In all the conversation on the way back to town we managed to avoid mentioning that we'd put in twelve hours, hiked between eight and ten rugged miles, and had blissfully walked away from the only rising trout we'd seen.

Of course, such stories never really end. We made plenty of points with the boys for even trying it ("You mean you went *up there?*") and handled it the way you deal with making a fabulous rifle shot while squirrel hunting: by acting as if we mountain men do this all the time, it's nothing. We also found the new lake on the map (it was there but lacked a name), went back twice, and caught some trout both times. They were rainbows, oddly enough, the results of airdrop stocking.

"What's your survival rate on airdrops?"

"Well, it's pretty good . . . when we hit the lake."

We took to calling it Lost Lake, for obvious reasons, but that's getting a little confusing. We call them all Lost Lake when other fishermen are within earshot. The high-lake anglers I know come in only two varieties: those who generously tell all but a

minor secret or two to whoever asks, and those of us who guard
what little we *do* know with psychotic skill.

Once high summer is on — the short but dependable season
lasting at least through most of July and August — things get
easier. That's not to say you'll always take fish, but because the
trout are feeding daily, you have a fair shot, which is all you can
reasonably ask for.

As I see it, the psychology of our local cutthroat is
paradoxical. The fish tend to feed opportunistically, the result of
lives passed in comparatively sparse waters where there may be a
fair diversity of insects and other food organisms but where
heavy hatches and other concentrations are rare — waters where
survival depends on a distinctly nonselective approach. The few
times I've killed and cleaned high-lake cutthroats, their stomachs
have contained a bouillabaisse of flying ants, beetles, caddis flies,
scuds, midges, snails, backswimmers, spinners, various nymphs
and pupae, maybe an odd leech, as well as the inevitable green
goo with legs and eyes in it that could be anything.

At the same time, they have a distinct retiring streak.
Cutthroats are not the shyest of trout (that distinction probably
goes to the golden), but they do seem to have a genetic
cautiousness, not to mention the ability to vanish so completely
you could swear the lake didn't have a fish in it. When they're
working, they are not often selective to fly pattern (with, of
course, the usual periodic exceptions without which the sport
would be no fun), but they can be maddeningly picky about
things like fly-line shadows on the water, speed and depth of
retrieval, and so on.

If the trout are up and working, you'll usually find them in
the shallows, the littoral zone where sunlight penetrates, aquatic
vegetation grows, insects and crustaceans thrive, and where most
of the transactions in the food chain take place. If they're rising
— that heart-lifting sight — you're in business. If not, they still
may be there, noodling around the bottom in a few feet of
water, picking up whatever they can find. It's not unusual to

find them concentrated along a certain shelf, against a drop-off, or at a stream inlet or outlet.

You look for them, walking back from the bank if you can, carrying the rod tip low, keeping your shadow off the water, peering through polarized glasses and keeping in mind that a trout is well camouflaged on the side he shows to eagles, ospreys, and fishermen.

Maybe they're *not* concentrated. Maybe they're everywhere, with rises and boils blanketing the lake, or maybe the only trout you see is sucking ants along a shady, overhung bank. You fish for them where you find them, but you have to find them first. Blind fishing in the dark water over the drop-off shelf is a last resort — sometimes profitable, usually not.

There's a local story about deep water in high lakes. A man hereabouts heard that one of the nearby subalpine lakes had been plumbed at something like eighty feet. With visions of 30-inch cutthroats in his head, he hauled a canoe in there, paddled to the center of the lake, lowered a large hook baited with half a sucker, and settled back to watch his bobber. After several fishless hours, he reeled in to check his bait, only to find his sucker meat frozen solid.

If the fish are feeding, they'll be in or near the shallow water. They'll also be moving, maybe fast, maybe slow, because there's no current to deliver the bugs except at the inlet and outlet. This means you have to cast to where they'll be, not to where they just were, leading them like you do a duck with a shotgun. This can be easier said than done.

With only the rarest exceptions, I fish nothing but wet flies in these lakes, regardless of what the fish are doing — wet flies just under the surface film when the trout are showing on top, or crawled along the bottom when they're working deep. The pattern hardly matters; the size matters some. A #14 seems like a good compromise. While it's big enough to be worth the trouble to bite, it's not so big as to be puzzling or even frightening. If they don't like it, I usually go down instead of up, to a #16 instead of a #12.

Did I say the pattern hardly matters? Let's say it hardly matters *objectively*. I'll use anything as long as it's a Hares Ear Soft Hackle, a Zug Bug or other peacock-bodied fly, a little tan midge pupa, a pink or olive scud, or one of a pair of small streamers. These are established personal favorites, not so much fly patterns as articles of faith generating much magic. I actually believe in the magic, but I try not to talk about it too much. People give me funny looks.

The rationale for wet flies in general is that a fish is more likely to take something that's right in front of his nose than something he has to move to the surface for. It seems logical and works for me most of the time, notwithstanding the fact that A. K. can fish right next to me and take them on dry flies.

I carry some other patterns, of course. I now have my high-lake selection down to two boxes, one containing flies I'll use and the other with flies I will *not* use. I have more than once caught cutthroats by fishing a Hares Ear Soft Hackle through a spinner fall, but it would never work if I didn't have some spinners along that I declined to use. It's like a friend of mine who couldn't stop smoking cigarettes until she started carrying a full pack in her purse. It's the same thing, or close to it.

Finally, there's the mood of the fish, the ultimate hieroglyphics in all this. When the conditions are right, the fish will feed, and when they're feeding you can probably catch a few, given a modicum of caution and a little bit of a feel for it. A hatch, spinner fall, mating flight of caddis flies, or a weed bed full of shrimp will help, and cloudy, cool, breezy, drizzly weather is better than a bright, warm, calm day.

Both are good bets, but neither is a guarantee. I have now and then caught scads of cutthroats on blistering, sunny days from glass-smooth water without a sign of a bug, having no idea why or much curiosity, either. One has one's theories, but it's hard to speculate in the face of success.

The crack high-country cutthroat fisher is a good hiker, a fair-to-middling caster, a poor aquatic entomologist, and a hands-down master of the educated guess and the long, quiet bank sit. He also needs a working sense of humor, even if at times he aims his jokes with the coldheartedness of a sniper.

What makes it all worthwhile is that the fish are cutthroats, the native trout of the Rocky Mountains, sometimes called just that: natives. The ones here are of the Yellowstone variety. I know that because they have large spots that are heavier towards the stern of the fish, and also because people who actually know about such things have told me that's what they are. If the spots were smaller and more evenly distributed, I'd say they were more like Snake River cutts, thus just about exhausting my expertise on the subject. There are many varieties of cutthroat (fifteen by one count), some common, others extremely rare, a few extinct, still others hybridized to the point of being generic. The taxonomic distinctions that mark them are usually too subtle for this basically simpleminded fisherman. I'm frankly more concerned with how big they are or where they live than with what kind they are.

Around here the cutts are not typically of magazine-cover-photo size. Trout in the 9- to, say, 12- or 14-inch class are the rule, though the wall hangers do show up. Wall hangers? Well, cutthroats in the 18- to 22-inch class come out of here every year, each one being newsworthy. Sometimes they fall into the hands of kids who haven't yet learned that these fish are impossible to catch, though more often they come to hard-working, careful anglers who have more than earned them. Most are taken somewhere in the 73,391 acres that comprise the Indian Peaks Wilderness Area, and I dare not say even what little more I know about that. You understand.

To put it in its proper perspective, if you release a 15- or 16-inch cutt, you have the right to whoop and scream and give your buddy a big, platonic kiss.

We Western fishermen tend to have a soft spot for the trout that evolved in these mountains, and fishing for natives, especially in what passses for wild country, constitutes a kind of regular pilgrimage. Cutthroats have an aura about them of being "out there" where the wind blows free, where men are men, and all the rest of that Western movie crap.

Interestingly, this is largely an illusion. The fact is, most of these lakes (not to mention the streams connecting them and the beaver ponds that come and go in the meadows) were devoid of trout of any kind a century ago. The few that *were* up there were greenbacks instead of Yellowstone cutts, and most of those were quickly fished out by civilized human beings, poisoned and/or smothered in mine tailings, or outcompeted by introduced species — the then-foreign and exotic brookies, browns, and rainbows. It's a chilling thought, all that water without trout.

The fish that are there now nearly all came from some stocking efforts, either by anonymous individuals, the Division of Wildlife, or the 73-year-old Boulder Fish and Game Club. The latter is a private group whose main activity involves backpacking fingerling cutthroats into remote alpine lakes.

Think about that for a minute.

The fish and game club is among those few organizations which, without newsletters, magazines, conventions, office space, general fanfare, or plaques commemorating the fact, are just quietly and efficiently *doing something*. It's refreshing. They work with the blessing and assistance of the Colorado Division of Wildlife and have benefited countless anglers, many of whom have never even heard of them.

Another trout you'll find in the wilderness, in two lakes and a few miles of stream, is the Emerald Lake rainbow. This is actually a natural cutthroat/rainbow hybrid that was introduced here recently because it spawns well in lakes, using both the inlets and the outlets, and otherwise does well and grows large in high-lake environments. A biologist connected with this project told me the fish can spawn in water as cold as 38 degrees, giving them a good jump on the short growing season. They look like rainbows (most of them, anyway), act like cutthroats, and fight as well as both put together, lacking only the rainbows' propensity for jumping. A wonderful fish.

The poor little greenback cutthroats, so beaten down they were once thought to be extinct, have now been reestablished a little ways north in Rocky Mountain National Park where, in a few areas, you can fish for them on a strictly catch-and-release basis.

This is a classic success story: a species of wild creature brought back from the brink of oblivion by a typically undermanned, underfunded group (the Greenback Trout Recovery Team), now more or less thriving in waters where they may not have lived originally but which are nonetheless within their native drainage.

There was some controversy recently over a string of beaver ponds in which the greenbacks were stocked up in Rocky Mountain National Park. The brook trout who were living there were poisoned out, and the rare cutthroats were stocked in their place. Fine, but before too long the brookies started showing up again. It was speculated that some enterprising angler had reintroduced the brook trout, but one member of the Recovery Team told me he thought they'd poisoned the brook trout too late in the fall, killing the fish themselves but leaving the fertile eggs.

In any case, the brookies came back and began to grow to large size, while at the same time the cutthroat population began to decline. Were the brookies growing large on a diet of little greenbacks? The evidence seemed to point to that, but the biologists said no, the more aggressive brookies were simply outcompeting the cutts.

After a closure of nine years, the ponds were reopened to sport fishing, partly to see how anglers responded to the cutthroats, but mostly as a means to remove the brookies without harming the greenback population. The regulations were flies and lures only, catch and release on the cutts, a regular limit on the brook trout.

Is there *always* a glitch in the system when it comes to fisheries management? It looked perfect on paper, but the one thing they didn't count on was that lots of fly-fishers would show up on the ponds, gentle, easygoing types who found it difficult to kill those big, beautiful brookies, even in the name of science.

Back at the parking lot, volunteers armed with clipboards were taking an angler's survey.

"How many fish did you catch?"

"Eight cutts and six brookies."

"May we see the brook trout?"

"Uh, we put 'em back."

"Groan . . ."

Most of the groans came from Bruce Rosenlund, head of the Recovery Team and a genuinely nice man. The unofficial slogan for the project became: "Kill a brookie for Bruce."

A fair number of the brook trout have been taken out now (they're delicious, by the way), but it doesn't seem to have helped the greenbacks much. In fact, with the big brooks pretty much "cleaned out" (a phrase I don't especially like), fishing pressure on the ponds has dropped. The greenbacks may be rare and exotic, but they have turned out to be a wimp fish: pretty enough, but small and poor fighters. I know some of the people on the Recovery Team and we all applaud their efforts, but I think they'll now admit that the greenback cutthroat is of more interest to the biologist than to the fisherman.

Backpack stocking, airdrop stocking, introduced and reintroduced species.

It may be that the concept of a place as being truly wild and untouched is no longer useful in areas like this. Whenever I'm up there and get myself into the standard quasi-mystical wilderness head, it's a sure sign I'm about to run into a mob of screaming kids, trip over a bean can, or be intruded upon by the whop-whop-whop of a helicopter — though it may well be a helicopter full of trout, and I always watch where it goes.

I was recently told that the Indian Peaks area annually entertains something like 95,000 visitors, which leads me to suspect that the United States government defines the word "wilderness" differently than I do. The same ranger who gave me that figure said the bears had been acting funny, something that seemed to puzzle him but that makes perfect sense to me. I've been acting a little funny myself lately.

The official map of the area is covered with various crosshatch patterns indicating no fires, no camping, no "recreational livestock" (otherwise known as horses). You need a permit to camp there; you can get it at the same place you get tickets for rock-and-roll concerts.

So much for the unspoiled wilderness, although I don't turn my nose up at having four or five species of trout where there was once only one — and precious few of those — nor can I quite bring myself to think of a once-empty lake that's now full of fish as having been "spoiled."

All of this has been necessary and I can't argue with it except to say that locals should have something like diplomatic immunity from all those permits and paperwork, and to point out that the powers that be may have brought a lot of their people-management problems on themselves. For what it's worth, a wildeness area should be handled as follows:

First, remove the "sanitary facilities," also known as outhouses, plow up the roads and parking lots, reseed the trails, and otherwise vacate the interior. Then build a dirt parking lot at the area boundary and erect the following sign:

Howling wilderness beyond this point
Caution
Bad weather
Rough terrain
Bears that act funny
No rescue facilities available
Enter at your own risk

Have a nice day

Naturally, there are ways to circumvent at least some of the
crowding problems. You can go to the more popular areas early
or late, before or after the brilliant summer days of endless sky
and gleaming snowcaps, when you're more likely to meet
only others like yourself — an aristocratic but useful device.

You can and should go on days with what, in another
circumstance, would be called "bad weather" — gray,
thundering skies, drizzle, wind, rain clouds pouring through the
passes like syrup. Tourists don't like that much and will run
squealing from it when it happens suddenly, as it often does.
The trout, on the other hand, seem to love it, rising and boiling
almost imperceptibly in the iron-blue choppy water. You fish on
the windward side of the lake where floating bugs collect and
where the wave action stirs up nymphs, casting into the breeze.
You do this after you've reached into your daypack for the wool
shirt, sweater, and rain gear that are always there, even in the
warmest, sunniest weather. You wait out lightning under cover
on lower ground. Lightning is the only outside force in the
mountains that is actually dangerous, regardless of how well
prepared you are, and a man standing out in the open, in the
water, waving a long stick is a prime candidate for termination.

You can avoid the big lakes with names and well-marked trails
and fish the anonymous blue spots on the maps around them,
lakes for which information is sometimes scarce. You can get
skunked in the most hideous way doing this: by not only failing
to catch or even see any trout, but by walking away with the
fretful intuition that they're in there anyway, doing whatever it is
cutthroats do when you can't find them. Thus, in your secret
heart, you can never really write off a lake, even if you never go
back.

If you do take fish, you keep your mouth shut except in the

most trusted company. This is a further advantage of releasing your catch — you can always claim failure. Just try to keep a straight face.

You can be aware that most human activity takes place along trails and within a few miles of official access points. Even in heavily used areas, there are lakes and stretches of stream that are hardly touched.

Remember also that wilderness areas and national parks draw heavily. Going farther than everyone else is one way to beat the crowds, but stopping short of the trailheads can also work. Follow the streams out into the less glamorous surrounding country.

You can stay home and do chores on weekends and major holidays.

Finally, you can learn to live with the fact that these lands belong to the people and that it shouldn't be surprising to find some of them walking around up there. You'll now and then run into folks with more guts than brains, but most people obey the rules and stay out of the more rugged areas. What it boils down to is, if I feel like I'm better than some of the people I meet on the lower trails stumbling along in smooth-soled street shoes, that's my problem; and if I disagree with some of the management programs, it's at least partly because I'm a radical with a radical's simple solutions. That, by the way, is not an apology.

So I hike and fish because it's pretty country and the trout are out there, with the red slashes on their jaws and their fine, efficient coloring that changes from lake to lake. I look for two things, mostly: trout and solitude, in that order.

CHAPTER NINETEEN

The Fly Box

FOR DAYS NOW IT'S
been bitter cold. Two nights ago it hit 61 degrees below zero in a
little Colorado mountain town I've never heard of before and
never will again unless I stumble on it someday. If I do, I'll
remember it because there will be a sign somewhere
memorializing the fact that it was there, in 1985, that the record
low temperature for the state was recorded. Summer tourists in
years to come will find it hard to imagine, so hard they won't
even try.

Closer to home, the firewood pile is shrinking too fast for a
week this far from spring, and snow tracked through the
workroom behind the kitchen doesn't melt. The river is frozen
bank to bank at the Island Pool.

It's good weather for inside chores, Mexican food and
German beer, piling on calories and numbness by way of
insulation. It was in weather like this a few years ago that a
woman shot her husband to death just up the road during what

the newspapers referred to as a "domestic dispute." I forget how the courts ruled on that one, but a local old-timer who understands such things declared that the gentleman had expired from a terminal case of the shack nasties.

It's too cold even for ice-fishing, and thoughts of *real* fishing can be distant and painful.

And then Chuck Digby called. Seems he'd been thinking about the new state lease on Terryall Creek just below the dam. Wanted to know if I'd like to go up there with him in the spring. He doesn't know anything about it except that it's been posted for years and is a tailwater. Might be good; might be outrageous.

"Love to," I said, pointing out that we could go in early June (still spring up there) when the pike will be moving in the reservoir. We could cast big Wooly Buggers and Zonkers for pike in the mornings, take a lunch and nap break, switch from 7- or 8-weight rods to 4s or 5s, and fish dry flies in the stream till dark. Then we could lounge around the campfire, maybe trying to whip up a simplified version of pike almondine.

Yeah, love to. As soon as spring comes.

Maybe A. K. would like to come along, though he doesn't think much of pike. When I pointed out to him once that northern pike not only take flies but are good to eat, he said, "Do me a favor, eat every one of the bastards you catch."

I might give him a call anyway. During a spell of weather like this, he'd agree to anything involving a fly rod and liquid water.

Chuck and I chatted for a while then about a soft-hackled, wet-fly dressing for the Brown Hackle Peacock, how to deal with leaks in waders (buying a new pair was mentioned), etc. And then the phone went dead. No doubt a starling had landed on a frozen wire, snapping it off clean.

Did I mention it's been cold?

I opened another beer and looked for a spot on my fishing agenda to pencil in "Terryall — trout and pike — early June." This legal-sized piece of yellow paper is already getting unintelligible, with frantically scribbled notations in several colors of ink and red pencil. Maybe I should type it up while I can still decipher most of what it says. Two or three months from now it will look like detailed instructions written in Arabic for summoning the devil.

Then again, why bother? It is, after all, just a device, symptomatic relief, something to do. I've already listed more trips than there's time for between April and October, even if some of that time didn't have to be dedicated to keeping body and soul together. The Terryall expedition will fit in nicely as long as there are seven weeks in June this year, but I don't want to dwell on this; it might sound like I'm going quietly mad.

I did mention it's been real cold lately, didn't I?

I'm more or less stranded here (the phone is dead and I feel in my bones that the truck won't start) so I think what I'll do is get back to the fly-tying. It's a quiet, absorbing inside job, I'll need the flies, and, best of all, in that context there isn't much time before the fishing season is in full swing — only about ten weeks. That's just about enough time to get all the fly boxes filled, working at something less than a feverish pace.

I've done a little tying already, but it's been in the research and development vein. There are a couple of possibilities, like an enormous, upside-down bass nymph and the simple wet-fly dressing for the Brown Hackle Peacock I was telling Chuck about, as well as a number of clear failures — ideas that just had to run their course, like a dose of the flu. This is how it begins for me. This is the season when grotesque ideas hatch and I find myself at the vise with visions of patterns that won't quite fit on the hooks. But at least I'm tying. Soon I settle down to refilling the boxes, more or less calmly, starting more or less at the beginning.

For me, the beginning is the Hares Ear Soft Hackle. I invented this fly a number of years ago in one of those forehead-slapping bursts of inspiration in which I saw that you could combine two of the best wet-fly patterns in the world into one, thus taking my place in the long line of other tiers who have also invented this fly. My only real claim to originality is that I use extension-cord-grade copper wire for the rib, instead of the traditional gold. I thought the copper color was more subtle and natural, an impression helped along by the fact that I had several miles of the stuff on hand.

I start with a debarbed Mustad 3906 hook wrapped liberally with lead fuse wire. I like them heavy. The body is dubbed fat and bristly with roughly blended hare's mask, ribbed with the copper. The hackle used to be brown partridge, but I've recently gone to Indian hen necks in light brown to dark ginger, with the dark badger marking down the quill. The partridge looks a bit more English, and therefore classier, but the hen is cheaper, easier to use, and comes in a wider range of sizes.

It's a fabulously ugly fly, cheap and quick to make, and very effective. I like flies that are so easy to replace that I can make those kamikaze, hook-the-fish-or-lose-the-fly casts without even the briefest of second thoughts. I'm as impressed as anyone with artistic fly-tying but, to be useful, flies must be thoughtlessly expendable.

The Hares Ear Soft Hackle passes for a caddis pupa (if you must think in those terms) but is in fact an all-purpose "bug" in the sense that a five-year-old kid would use that word. I think five-year-old kids and game fish view the world in much the same way: both are capable of intense, single-minded observation, but they see the essence of a thing rather than the details.

I now dedicate an entire, small box to these flies because I go through so many of them. I started last season with eleven or twelve dozen in sizes 10 through 16, and when I sat down to tie this winter, I had almost nothing but #10s left. In a fit of off-season ruthlessness, I dumped all the 10s in the bluegill box and set out to tie a dozen dozen in sizes 12 through 20. This was done in the belief that changing sizes (usually going down instead of up) is more likely to be the answer to a fishing problem than changing *patterns*. With a fly like this that doesn't imitate anything in particular, you are freed from the insectile chauvinism that dictates, for instance, that all Blue-winged Olives shall be 16s, 18s, and 20s. You can make them any size you want.

Dumping or relegating flies is best done during the coldest week of the year, when you're as close to being objective as you'll ever get. Flies that have stayed in a box for even a single season are probably useless and should move aside — the only exceptions being things like the Brown Drakes that are just waiting for their owner to hit that damnably unpredictable hatch on the Seven Castles Pool.

While I'm on the wet flies, I'll whip up a few dozen of that Soft Hackle Peacock pattern. It's nothing more than a weighted 3906 hook with a peacock herl body and a long, sparse, mottled-brown hackle, another simple dressing that looks buggy, will probably catch fish, and is considerably easier to tie than the Zug Bug.

Whether this fly will actually replace the Zug Bug in seasons to come is yet to be determined. I plan to do considerable field testing this coming summer, but replacing an old established pattern with a new one is a matter in which practicality is only one of the variables that needs to be weighed. The Zug Bug and I go back a long way and, although I can be ruthless, I find it difficult to be coldhearted.

Whatever happens, I'll never be without some peacock herl-bodied nymph or wet fly. There's something about that material that even heavily fished-for trout find fascinating, and I've finally figured out how to tie it so it doesn't fall apart after two fish. All you do is tie in a few strands of herl along with one length of wire (gold, copper, it hardly matters because it hardly shows). Then you twist them together, making a kind of wire and herl chenille which holds up under all kinds of abuse. This is another of my new discoveries that, I'm told, has been in use for going on a century.

Before I move on to the Adams box, I'll probably replace the missing scud patterns. I use the basic Glad Bag Shrimp tie in two sizes and two colors (10s and 12s, in dirty olive and pink).

The rest of the nymph box doesn't look too bad, although I'll need a few more little Olives and dark quill bodies. This kind of thing comes under the heading of "fill-ins" and can be done last, or at the last minute, or not at all, whichever comes first. The rock worms, Drake nymphs, Golden stone nymphs, and a few others will get filled up on three or four consecutive nights of tying a half dozen of these and four or five of those — the kind of sessions that leave the desk littered with eighteen different materials and five colors of thread. It's an inevitable mess into which the scissors will vanish late in the evening.

Since the Salmon Fly hatch on the Colorado River eluded me last year, the big black stone nymphs and elk-hair dries are intact. It's disturbing to have an entire box — albeit a specialty box — come through a whole season without a single casualty. Where's that fishing agenda? "Stone flies — Colorado — April." This is now written in red pencil, underlined, in what passes for a margin, with an arrow sticking it in between bluegills, crappies, spawning rainbows, and what seems to say "pre-runoff browns — St. Vrain." I've got to either type this thing up or throw it away.

Next comes the Adams box. Ah, the Adams, the finest of dry flies, everyone's favorite, a triumph of expressionism. I tie what's been called the Western Adams: identical to the standard tie except with a moose-hair instead of a hackle-fiber tail. I see I'll need a few more each in sizes 14 through 20. The Adams is the only other fly I carry that has a box all to itself which, apparently, is the highest recommendation I can give. I tend to be a presentationist when it comes to dry flies, figuring that the Adams will work nine times out of ten when the trout are looking up. (When they're looking down, they probably want a Hares Ear Soft Hackle.)

This is an idea you'll arrive at if you do most of your fishing on Western freestone creeks, like I do. The three forks of the St. Vrain, the Fall, the Thompson, Glacier Creek, the Cache La Poudre — all Adams streams.

A few years ago I got on a Poudre River jag, went up there about every other week all summer and fall. Under a bridge about halfway up the canyon road there was a tree stump, complete with the roots, that had washed down in the spring runoff. This thing was a natural sculpture. At first glance, and even for a second or two afterwards, it looked exactly like a fly-fisherman frozen in mid-backcast. The first time I saw it, I even said to the person sitting next to me in the cab of the pickup, "There's a guy fishing that bridge hole." There was a short moment of disorientation while the changing angle of the pickup turned the thing back into a piece of wood. In fact, it didn't look much like a fly-caster at all. There was just something suggestive about the solid form with a rodlike root sticking up behind it. A bare suggestion in the right place at the right time.

All that season, every time I saw that thing, there was a flash of erroneous recongnition, even after I knew what it was — a few seconds of "guy fishing the bridge hole." I was fooled time and again, always for about the same amount of time it takes for a dry fly to float over a fish rising in fast water.

That stump looked less like a fly-fisherman than an Adams looks like a bug, and I like to think I'm a little smarter than the average trout. Still, I expected to see a fly-fisher along a trout stream, so that's what I saw. And that's why I fish the Adams.

This is a belief, a kind of faith, that proves itself often enough to be comfortable but not quite often enough to be the whole truth. It comes from doing a lot of fishing in a certain kind of water and also from a view of the world as a place where success ought not to depend on absolute, nitpicking, legalistic accuracy, even though sometimes it does.

Luckily fly-fishing is one area of human endeavor where you can cherish conflicting beliefs simultaneously. To that end I like to be able to match the hatch with Blue-winged Olives, Blue

Duns, Blue Quills, Red Quills, Pale Morning Duns, Ginger
Quills, various emergers; little Brown, Black, and Yellow stone-
flies (which can also pass for midges), Pale Morning Duns,
Speckled, Rusty, and Michigan Chocolate spinners; plus a box of
various and sundry wet and dry midges in assorted sizes, colors,
and patterns. Some of the floating midges even sport trailing
pupal shucks.

There are caddis dries of the down-wing, elk-hair variety, as
well as palmer-hackled, "fluttering" types, and in that same box
reside some Humpies, Royal Wulffs, ants, and beetles.

All of these will need at least some attention, as will the
hoppers, which I almost forgot because I can't find any. They're
all used up. I can't find any unaccounted-for comparments,
either, so where did I keep my hoppers last season?

This mystery, plus the addition already of the Brown Hackle
Peacock wet, plus the planned addition of the March Brown dry
make it clear that about halfway through this winter's tying I'll
have to get into the yearly reorganizaion of the fly boxes. This is
an annual attempt at some kind of order that means it will be
mid-July before I can just reach into the pocket in the vest that
hides the fly I want without fumbling.

For roughly a decade now I've been working to simplify and
focus my fly selection, a project that inevitably requires a new fly
box or two every season. I can't figure that out. Andy Rooney,
my favorite nonfishing columnist, has said that no new law
should be made without an old law being thrown out to make
room for it. That's how I feel about fly patterns, but laws and
trout flies are among those things in life that resist being made
sense of.

Then there is the streamer box. At the moment it holds
nothing but Tricolors and Mickey Finns, which means the
Muddler Minnows, Brown and White Bucktails, Black Wooly
Buggers, and Gierach Specials will all need to be tied. A Gierach
Special is tied thusly: a body of Pearl flashabou piping is wound
on a weighted, long-shanked streamer hook. The beard is sparse

white bucktail tied just past the bend of the hook. The wing is a medium bunch of gray-squirrel tail tied just a tad longer than the beard, with a topping of six or eight strands of pearl flashabou under six or eight strands of peacock herl. The head is salmon-egg-red with black-on-white painted eyeballs. I started out humbly referring to this as the Gray Squirrel Streamer, but the first time someone called it a Gierach Special my ego kicked in and I jumped on the name. Wouldn't you?

That's about it except for the inevitable experiments which will go into the odd box, alongside some patterns that are in a kind of purgatorial limbo somewhere between the trout selection, the panfish selection, and the local Trout Unlimited raffle.

I almost forgot the Tan-bodied Adams, a little perversion of the standard tie that does well in the mountain brook trout and cutthroat streams. The standard Adams would probably work as well, but this is something I came up with myself, being, in typical angler's fashion, simultaneously mired in tradition and constantly dissatisfied with things as they are. For that matter, there are surely a few others I've forgotten and will think of as they come along, not to mention the additional impulsive changes and additions. As much as I'd like to have everything down pat, a fly selection is an everchanging thing. In one sense at least, it's a model of the angler's mind, so mine is, as you'd expect, somewhat cluttered and disorganized.

This may be one of those winters when all the flies actually get tied, giving each box its brief, glorious moment of looking like an illustration in an Orvis catalog. It won't last, just as waders eventually leak and hair turns gray, but that's okay. Flies are lost over fish and life goes on.

Actually, the first flies to leave the neat, new ranks won't go to fish or bushes but to the home-water box. This is the single box I try to carry on expeditions to local, well-known waters in an ongoing act of ascetic bravado. It's the sparse selection of dries, wets, and streamers that usually catch fish hereabouts if you're doing all the other things right — a slight extension of the Adams and Hares Ear fixation. It's beginning to look like this year's reorganization will leave the Perrine #100 fly box (a 4 x 6-inch poor man's Wheatley) free to take the place of the smaller home-water box, allowing room for the addition of some hoppers and midges that, at the appropriate times of year last season, had to be taken along in a separate box.

There are only two problems here. First, even a small lapse in an exercise in simplicity is like giving up cigarettes and then slowly but surely starting up again. In other words, a lost cause.

Second, the Perrine #100 doesn't quite fit any of the pockets of the official fishing shirt that replaces the vest on short, local trips. It does, however, fit in the pockets of the light, Vietnam-style camouflage jacket that was bought for turkey hunting but may well become next summer's fishing shirt. I'm not much into brand loyalty, so my only hesitation here is that camouflage, once worn only by turkey hunters, duck hunters, and the active military, may these days be interpreted as a bold fashion statement.

So much for the trout flies. The bass and pike selection doesn't look too bad. There are plenty of flies in those two big boxes and hanging on the sheepskin hatband, looking at me with big, teddy-bear eyes and waving with rubber legs, though I guess I could use a few more clipped deer-hair frogs, and tying up a few of those 5-inch-long streamer contraptions that use half a pound of lead wire and half a rabbit skin is, if nothing else, therapeutic after constructing dozens of #26 midge pupae.

The empty spaces in the boxes mean fish fished for, and sometimes caught, last season, and work now. But it's good work, as good as any, better than most. Though I first started tying flies as nothing more than an economic necessity, I now see it as an integral part of the sport. I'm not a complete purist in this regard, having been known to buy flies when that was the easiest thing to do. Catching trout on Mike Lawson's Green Drakes is completely satisfactory, though I'm just noticeably happier using my own.

At the moment I'm well into the Hares Ear Soft Hackles, nearly finished with the #16s and at my comfortable cruising speed of just over a dozen flies per hour. It's a familiar pattern, so halfway through the #12s I had remembered all the tricks. Now all I have to do is adjust the pinch of dubbing when I change sizes; otherwise I'm on automatic. This is when the memories take hold — an old, favorite pattern is heavy with memories.

These flies caught bluegills, pumpkinseeds, rock bass, and crappies on those first, wild, 30- and 40-fish days in spring. Later they took browns and rainbows when fished deep in the rivers and, hand twisted slowly just under the surface of the high lakes, they hooked brookies and cutthroats, and brookies and cutts again in the beaver ponds. Whitefish have bitten them and so have grayling. I can see fish, hear water, smell pine. Last season something like 130 of these flies went the way of all flesh.

It's night. I'm sitting three feet from an uncurtained window that is radiating a black, deep-space cold into the room. The dog slept at my feet for a while, but has now moved to a spot closer to the stove. The old homestead feels remote. Still, it's the long downslope of winter now, as evidenced by the fact that I'm hard at work, tying another season's flies. The visions that were memories this morning have turned around to address the future as schemes.

At two hours, two beers, and three-dozen flies, I take a break. The dog looks up sleepily as I push the chair back. "You need to go out?" I ask. By way of an answer he groans and lays his head back down as if to say, "It's the middle of the night and cold as hell, why don't you go to bed?"

CHAPTER TWENTY

On the Road

THIS WAS SUPPOSED TO be an on-the-spot report from somewhere in Montana — one of the spring creeks or maybe the Missouri River, if the weather held. It's the last week in October, and Gary LaFontaine had invited me up to sample some of the not so well-known but sometimes fabulous late-season Montana fishing. As I'd never fished Montana this late, I jumped at the chance, even though I knew that an extended trip at this time of year involves something like a crap game with the weather. When I asked Gary what to bring, he said, "A light rod, a heavy rod, and lots of warm clothes."

I had the warm clothes packed — layers of cotton, chamois, wool, canvas, and down that I could wear all at once if I had to — but the crap game never even got started. I'd been watching the weather maps for a week, and they were starting to look grim. I'm no meteorologist, but I know what those big black lines and arrows mean. Sure enough, the night before I was supposed to leave, I got the call from Gary.

"Cash in your ticket; the Siberian Express is coming."

The Siberian Express isn't a passenger train; it's a storm that comes right down from the Arctic Circle to slam that open Montana country with gale winds, freezing temperatures, and horizontal snow. A storm that will make the national news. "Schools and businesses were closed all over Montana yesterday as a major winter storm entered the state," etc.

I guess I'd seen it coming, but my mind still groped around frantically for something to grab on to, even though I knew deep down that a trip into that would mean, at best, a week spent sleeping on a hard bench in a small airport. When we'd first talked about this trip, Gary had said he was as macho as anyone but that he drew the line at fishing in conditions that could be dangerous, and as we talked on the phone that night (rescheduling the trip for spring), I thought of something A. K. had said on the same subject.

"I enjoy fishing too much to risk my life at it. Death can really cut into your fishing time."

Okay, fair enough. I was beaten by logic and reasonableness, but I didn't feel good about it; I've actually been accused of being *un*reasonable on the subject of fishing trips. As we talked, I kept eyeing my gear, stacked ready to go, next to the door. There was a light rod and a heavy rod — a 7½-foot 4 weight and a 10-foot 8 weight — as well as the 8½-foot 5 weight I take everywhere these days and usually end up using. Clothes, vest, and waders were stuffed in a duffel bag with the wooden landing net snugged in the middle of everything to keep it from getting crushed. The cameras and film, along with reels, spare spools, and some extra leader material, were in a small daypack. The daypack would fit in the duffel, but I would have carried it on the plane, making my usual scene about not letting the cameras and film get X-rayed. It's a scene that immediately brands me as a terrorist, but I've gotten used to it. And anyway, how many P.L.O. types would hijack a flight from Denver, Colorado to

Missoula, Montana? ("Take me to Last Chance, Idaho, or I'll waste the stewardess.")

I could picture the flies. There was the usual stuff, heavy on the little mayflies and midges for the spring creeks, and a whole box of big, ugly, heavily weighted streamers for those 20-pound browns on the Missouri. Or were they supposed to be rainbows? I won't find out this year.

I had my feet propped up on the desk, there was a nice fire going in the stove, and I was holding a beer in one hand and scratching the dog with the other. I figured the dog to be about the length and weight of one of those monster Missouri River trout. My heart was breaking.

When I finally hung up I immediately went into a state somewhere between jet lag and culture shock. For the last week I'd been slowly but surely working myself into an on-the-road head, preparing myself for the jolts my system would have to take from hurtling north in a plastic-and-chrome projectile that, by all rights, shouldn't fly, and then, only hours after my arrival, finding myself standing in a trout stream amid wind, water, ducks, trout, trees, mayflies, and the famous Big Sky you're always reading about on license plates.

It would have been weird, but I was ready for it — the jammed parking lot and crowded airport in Denver, sticking out like a misfit in a Woolrich shirt, blue jeans, and hiking boots in the middle of all those tired businessmen in suits.

I've always thought there was some obscure religious significance in the fact that you sometimes have to get right in the thick of it in order to get away from it, an impression that's heightened by my dislike of flying, a dislike that, to be honest, borders on fear. I'll fly when there's a good trout stream in the deal, but I don't like it. They say the bigger planes are safer, but I figure the bigger ones are *heavier*.

There are people in my life who sometimes worry about me when I go off into the fields and streams, not realizing that the country is a calm, gracious, forgiving place and that the real dangers are found in the civilization you have to pass through to get there. When I take off on a trip I always think, Please, if I'm going to get killed on this one, let it be on the way back, after I've caught some fish.

This state of what you'd have to call negative culture shock (emotional exhaustion caused by *not* going somewhere) seemed to be another subtle way of getting cheated by the world, not unlike getting venereal disease from a toilet seat. I put another log in the stove, opened another beer, and consoled myself. There had, after all, been other trips.

Less than two months before I'd been on the San Juan River in New Mexico with Ed Engle. I'd driven down to Durango on a bright, cool, August day — an uneventful nine-hour trip more or less right down the spine of the Colorado Rockies — following directions I'd gotten from Ed's wife, Monica. They were lovely directions. She didn't know the numbers of the highways, but she knew the rivers: "Go down to Golden and turn west like you were going to the South Platte, then keep going at Pine Junction like you were going to the Tomahawk lease. Take the turn for Buena Vista like you were going to the Arkansas . . ." and so on to Del Norte at the North Fork of the Rio Grande and then over to Durango, crossing the Piedra, Los Pinos, Dolores, and Animas rivers. Thank you, Monica, I don't know the names of the roads either.

The idea was to do a fishing tour of the Southwest part of Colorado, an area I'd fished only once a long time ago, but this was a record wet year for the state, and all the rivers were too high and muddy to fly-fish. That evening Ed told me that "Animas" was short for a yard-long Spanish name meaning "The River of Lost Souls" and that the Dolores was "The River of Despair." It seems every time the Spanish explorers discovered a river, someone fell in and drowned. Moral: don't try to wade a river wearing armor.

And, as I'd noticed driving over them, they were muddy. Rivers of lost souls and despair indeed.

So, we ended up over the New Mexico line on the San Juan, a tailwater stream below the Navajo Dam that would be, if nothing else, clear.

It was clear, alright, and full of big trout that a guy could catch with some regularity if he was careful. It was also jammed with other Colorado fishermen who, like Ed and I, had come south to escape the mud. There were also plenty of locals on the water, and it wasn't long before we realized we'd waded into something of a cultural clash.

The first stretch of river below Navajo Dam is designated catch and release, the second stretch has a limit of one fish over 18 inches (I understand that's recently been raised to 20 inches), and below that it's a regular limit. The special-regulation water is restricted to barbless flies and lures only, and when you take your one fish in that second stretch, you're through fishing for the day. This rule is designed to keep people from stringing up an 18-inch trout, only to switch it for a bigger one later on, a procedure that almost invariably results in the useless death of the first fish. In spite of the regulations, there was a fair amount of that going on.

Most of the out of staters were well-dressed, well-equipped, catch-and-release fishing types, while most of the locals were clad in work clothes, fishing spinning rods, and looking for that one legal fish. The common greeting was, "any keepers?" For the record, most of the fishermen there were acting within the law, though some were more than a little discourteous, but we did witness several flagrant violations. The award goes to the man who took a 20-inch rainbow in the catch-and-release water, strung it up, lashed the stringer to his ankle, and waded down into the one-fish-limit water, limping badly and looking guilty as hell.

There was no real trouble, but there were a lot of evil looks exchanged. Ed and I, dressed rather shabbily but nonetheless fly-fishing with snazzy tackle, were at one time or another given the hairy eyeball by just about everyone on the river.

It was a little strange, but, oddly enough, there is a distinct lack of emotion connected to those memories. We caught trout — big ones — and quickly accepted both the meat hunters and the snobs as facts of life, like mosquitos. The fact is, I can get just as aggravated with fishermen who are *more* snotty than I am instead of less so and it may be, in the final analysis, that there are only two kinds of anglers: those in your party and the assholes.

Now, only a few months later, what I remember about that trip are the trout — up to 4 pounds on flies down to #16 — and the typically wild, circuitous, convoluted conversations Ed and I have always had together. The talk after a good day on a good river seems brilliant and probably *is* brilliant in context, especially between two fishermen who go back together farther than either of them can clearly remember — all the way back to live bait. It's the talk of two old friends, men who are no longer exactly young but who are not yet old farts, though some of the early signs are there — talk that might just indicate the beginnings of something like shared wisdom. Of course, I don't remember much of what was said now, which only means we'll have to do it all again soon.

It's funny how the details you remember from a trip so often seem to be of superfluous things. The fishing from that New Mexico trip is filed solidly in my mind and in five boxes of Kodachrome slides, but one of my clearest recollections is of a half-hour lunch break in the town of Saguache (pronounced "so-watch"), Colorado, I ate in one of those "Cafe Eat" places across the street from the old historic jailhouse and museum. The food was excellent and the cook/waitress/probably owner felt compelled to point out, "You ain't from around here." A statement, not a question.

No ma'am, I ain't, and what's so memorable about that I'll never know, except that it's all bound up in the headlong romance of a road trip.

I still do most of my traveling by car, mostly by choice, sometimes through economic necessity. Even with all their failings, automobiles still have it over airplanes because they're attached to the ground and because in them you experience the subtle changes in the countryside, see wildlife, get stiff legs, and feel deliciously far from home.

When you're in the country, which is still most of the time here in the West, you get to stop now and then at those wonderful joints, the taverns, cafes, gas stations, and sprawling combinations thereof. These places are usually unremarkable from the outside except that they look lived in, with their collections of trailers, abandoned chicken coops, smokehouses, retired pickup trucks, and outbuildings of indeterminate purpose. The sign out front might say just about anything, but the classic is, "GAS WORMS COLD BEER."

Like most things that fall under a single heading, no two are exactly alike, but there are some similarities between them. For instance, none of them are Orvis shops, but virtually all of them sell supposedly humorous postcards with fishing themes. Some are more friendly to strangers than others, but all of them lack that brightly lit sterility of the so-called convenience stores.

Those of us who have fished for a long time grew up around places like this and hatched some of our early dreams amid their dusty displays of outdated, cheap tackle, poorly tied flies, and spools of monofilament made brittle by time. The worst of them simply fill our momentary needs for gas, coffee, and other forms of go-juice, but the best of them — the ones with hound dogs sleeping in front of the doors — are friendly, cozy repositories of local history, the kind of oral tradition that elevates average deeds and fair-to-middling-sized fish to the status of legend. We can spot them a mile away for the simple reason that they are outposts of the subculture to which we belong. You know you

can go in wearing hip boots and they'll just figure you've been
fishin' or irrigatin'.

They can spot us just as easily, even when they've never seen
us before and probably won't again. There's obviously something
about the excited energy if you're going and the profound
philosophical calm if you're coming back, not to mention the
fact that, though no one actually fishes in tweeds anymore,
fishing clothes are usually just a cut above regular work clothes.

There are other clues. Once, coming back from a trip to
Southern Idaho, I stopped in at a little joint for something or
other that I didn't really need but wanted to play with on the
road, maybe a cigar, or a cup of coffee. When I payed for it, the
woman behind the counter asked, "How was the fishing?"

"The fishing was fine," I said, and then, out of genuine
curiosity, added, "How did you know I'd been fishing?"

"Wet dollar bill," she answered, without looking up from her
newspaper.

The joints I'm talking about are seldom on the main drags,
and many of those that are have diluted whatever real character
they once had with too much "Howdy, Y'all" cuteness and too
many genuine Wyoming jackalope mounts. The good places are
often on what *used* to be the main drag before that new four-lane
was built and are the remnants of the once great herds of these
things that inhabited the country roads near the fishable waters
of America. Like fishermen, they're a little out of synch — on
roads that, to the uninitiated, don't seem to go anywhere. Some
of them would be pitiful if they didn't have that vague sense of
dignity about them, and when I see one boarded up I know it
will never be replaced by anything like the real article.

I love them, but I wouldn't care to own one.

I remember a place in Montana, somewhere along the Madison
River, that is fixed in my mind as the archetypal worms-and-
cold-beer store, Western style. The four of us were lost, three
back in the camper, one up in the lead car. We were driving up
and down a dirt road in the dark looking for a certain cutoff

that would put us at a certain place on the river, a little dirt
track through the trees that had eluded our lead man for the
better part of the evening.

Finally we turned in at a joint — a neon beer sign glimmering
through the darkness — to ask where the hell we were.
Stretching and blinking in the unlighted gravel parking lot, I
could hear the quiet but powerful sound of the Madison and
could just make out the dilapidated outbuildings (once actually
used for something, now filled with old horse tack and rusty
tools that will someday be unearthed by archeologists).

The inside was cluttered and a little smoky, with moths
attacking the overhead lights. The few trays of flies were of
better quality than usual (this was Montana, remember), and
there were several enormous old fish mounts on the walls:
rainbows, brown trout, and the obligatory monster whitefish.
Two guides were playing for money on a lumpy, quarter-slot
pool table.

How did I know at a glance they were guides? Well, there
were the clothes (faded chamois, bandanas), the leathery tans,
the uniform age (late 20s), the bulging biceps from rowing float
boats, the professionally cavalier attitude towards trout and
trout fishing which somehow seems to throw arcs of conspiracy
between the men and the fish on the walls, the level, appraising
gaze at the four of us "sports" as we walked in, and an indistinct
something (possibly an aroma) that said, these men are hard as
nails, competent, use colorful language, drink a bit but can hold
it, will fight if they have to (fairly if they can) but only when
properly provoked, have a working, functional sense of humor
and, in the finest grassroots existential tradition, don't give a
good God damn about much of anything, thank you very much.
They were fishing guides all right, no doubt about it.

It was one of these gentlemen who gave us the directions we
needed. They were accurate. Strangers don't often get a lot of
free, voluntary information in places like this, but what they *do*
get is usually fair and honest, as if some secret sign had been

passed.

Trips. There's something about throwing the gear in the
pickup or, rarely, in an airplane, and *going* that plugs into our
national consciousness as well as into that sublime craziness we
discover in adolescence and carry through the rest of our lives,
like it or not. Every generation since civilization began has
thought they invented sex and leaving home. In a way, they all
did. Voluntarily packing up and leaving home never quite loses
its charm. And sex . . . Well, you know.

Just to be on the road is good in a deep American way, but to
be on the road going fishing is almost too good for words.
You're exposed, extended, on a scent. Maybe you're going to a
favorite place you know to be good, or a place you've *heard* is
good, or maybe noplace in particular, like "Wyoming." Things
are in perspective because you're on your way to seriously and
diligently pursue success in an endeavor where success doesn't
matter in any normal way. Whatever happens, you will come
back without fish.

A trip is an adventure, and on an adventure things should be
allowed to happen as they will. Still, I have developed some
guidelines.

Bad camp cooks are okay as long as you can keep them away
from the food, but bad cooks who mix cans of spaghetti and
chile together in the same pan as a way of continuing to punish
their mothers for something should be avoided, as this tendency
may show up in nonculinary areas as well.

Whiners of all sorts should not come along. People who
cannot deal with the standard adversities — either real or
imagined — can throw a serious clod in the churn.

Compulsive score keepers should be avoided: people who
refuse to have had a good day unless they've hit some
preconceived mark, like "25 fish boated" or "at least one 20-
incher."

Never go fishing with someone else's kid unless you enjoy kids a lot more than you do fishing.

People who claim to own "fishing dogs" are all blinded by love. There's no such thing as a good fishing dog. Most of these beasts are retrievers who think they can do to trout what they've been trained to do to ducks. It may sound cute, but it's not. Stay away from people who take their dogs fishing.

Do not go fishing with someone who is so set on being back at a certain time that he will refuse to invent a case of car trouble to keep you on the water an extra day.

Don't travel in large or even medium-sized groups. A typical gang of six fishermen will include a bad cook, a whiner, a score keeper, someone who absolutely has to be back by Thursday noon, his five-year-old son, and his dog, Gonzo.

In the end, it's probably best to travel with established fishing partners, no more than two at a time. The old hands are like your regular brand of beer — less than perfect, perhaps, but predictable.

And never say exactly when you'll be back; that way it's not possible to be late.

Money is seldom a problem between friends, but to avoid confusion it's a good idea to have everyone put a certain amount of dough ($50, $150, depending on the trip) into an envelope marked "kitty." Group expenses come from the kitty, while personal expenses come from the pocket of the person in question. If there's anything left in the kitty at the end of the trip, it gets divided equally; if it runs out too soon, you all ante up again.

Try to eat and sleep reasonably well and don't whoop it up too much, while bearing in mind that a *little* whooping is unavoidable and probably necessary.

Fishing trips involve certain rituals, not the least of which is packing. For easy local jaunts, I have it down now to where I can be out the door, fully armed, in no more than five minutes, starting from a dead stop. I have a mantra that I recite:

"rodreelvestwaderscamera," and I never forget anything. Once
the season in under way, I usually have a broken-down rod, with
reel attached, lying conveniently on a table near the door, and I
can be on the St. Vrain River across the street almost the instant
the inclination strikes. I once thought about leaving a 7½-foot, 4-
weight strung up on the porch through the summer but was
warned by a well-known rod maker that if I did that it would
take major surgery to unseat the ferrules in the fall.

Longer trips of course seem to require more extensive
planning. The preparation for, say, a ten-day trip to Southern
Idaho can be a logistical chess game in which the possible
usefulness of every piece of fishing gear, camping gear, and
clothing you own is weighed in the days before your departure.
The final decision depends, as much as anything, on the size of
the vehicle you're traveling in.

In addition to everything else, trips to strange or notoriously
tricky waters require the presence of a fairly substantial fly-tying
kit filled with bits and scraps of fur and feathers gathered from
at least three continents with examples of Norwegian and English
metallurgy, most of which you won't use but wouldn't feel
comfortable without.

I've done a good deal of traveling with A. K. who, being a
professional flytier, has a much better travel kit than mine. At
least once on every trip I find myself saying something like,
"Arch, you got any hooks?"

So far I've never forgotten anything vital on a trip. I tend to
err in the other direction, hauling along things I have no earthly
use for, like five rods besides the one I'm going to be fishing
with.

This is another advantage to traveling in an automobile of
some sort — you can carry a lot more junk. You can also keep
an eye on it. An airline is much more likely to smash, lose, or
reroute your stuff than you are. No, it's never happened to me,
but I've heard all the horror stories.

Another thing I don't like about airplanes is the level of culture shock they inevitably produce. Travel shouldn't be that fast, that antiseptic, or that easy. My mind has not entered the late Twentieth Century sufficiently to be able to translate time spent sitting in a sealed capsule with distance covered. When I step into the thing in Denver and step out of it somewhere else, I feel like I've gotten to a place without actually *going* there in any kind of reasonable way.

A lot of modern human beings have gotten used to it, and I suppose *I* could get used to it too, though I'm not sure I want to.

Of course, culture shock on the outward-bound end of a trip is softened by the directional energy of "going fishing." Ultimately it will be you, your fly rod, and some trout, mackinaw, pike, or whatever, and that, at least, makes sense. Whatever strangeness there is to the place penetrates your aura of purposeful concentration at an acceptable rate. When it hits me the hardest is on the way back, when I'm tired and my sense of purpose has dissolved.

It happened a few years ago when three companions and I flew into Canada's Northwest Territories to spend a week in a fishing camp on a remote lake. We flew from Denver to Winnipeg, stayed overnight in a hotel that was much too posh for a gang of fishermen, and, at dawn the next morning, were driven to the airport to be loaded onto some kind of World War II transport — a DC-3 maybe. I don't know planes. All I know is the thing was sitting at enough of an angle that you had to climb the aisle, and I remember peeking into the cockpit, expecting to see John Wayne at the controls.

This lumbering old crate flew us north to a place called Stony Rapids, the last settlement in that direction. Next stop, the Arctic Circle.

From the dirt airstrip at Stony Rapids, we walked down to the river to catch the single-engine float planes that would take us two hundred-some miles farther north into North America's last great wilderness.

At the end of the third flight in the space of two days, I was found to be seized-up, frozen like a rabbit in the headlights of a car, and had to be pried from the plane by the guides when we arrived at the camp.

I soon got my color back, though, because I was on the ground — safe for the moment — and because the place was familiar enough: coniferous forests, lakes, streams, ducks, mosquitos, more of it than I was used to, but otherwise the same old stuff. The guides even spoke English, albeit Canadian English, where every sentence begins with "You know" and ends with "Eh?"

The only floral or faunal incongruity involved the wolves. I remember once stepping outside to relieve myself in the middle of the short, Northern night, hearing a wolf go off like an air-raid siren at what seemed to be very close range, and deciding it could wait until morning.

It was a fine trip, as expeditions into the real backcountry typically are. The catching of fish was nicely balanced against the not catching of fish to produce the proper level of drama, and it was all set against a backdrop of wonderful, wild loneliness.

What was hard on my mind, culture shock-wise, was the brutal unreality of the return trip. I woke up one morning in a comfortably rough camp in the territories and ate supper that night in an expensive hotel dining room in downtown Winnipeg.

Back up in the room, the boys were watching television — there were gunshots from snub-nosed revolvers, car chases, lots of griping and yelling. It was a bit too much, so I did what any seasoned outdoorsman would do: I took my small wad of exotic Canadian money down to the bar. In our week in camp I'd developed a taste for a certain brand of inexpensive Canadian beer, and I figured about fifteen of them would ease my troubled mind.

I was deep in an internal fog, so I was on my second beer before I realized something like a wedding reception was in progress. I was the only one there not in a tuxedo or an evening gown. I was dressed in week-old fishing clothes and, in spite of the fact that the place was jammed, I was all alone at the bar.

There was a group playing under blue lights at the far end of the large room, and they sounded strangely familiar, so familiar that I began to study them and, two beers later, realized, "My God! It's the Ink Spots!"

Now I wouldn't even be old enough to remember the Ink Spots except that they were my father's favorite group. He played their records all through my childhood and once told me how he and Ma had listened to them before they were married, when she was in high school and he was jerking sodas at a drugstore. He used to make some fantastic ice-cream concoction called the "Gierach Special" and probably never dreamed that his boy, years later, would also make Gierach Specials, except that mine would be trout flies.

It doesn't sound like much now. There was only one guy in the band old enough to have been an original member — the lead singer was about my age — but it was the Ink Spots, all right. It even said so on the bass drum.

Somehow it was what I was looking for, a connection of some kind. I remember thinking, okay, it's over, I'm back.